THE GUILTLESS GOURMET goes ETHNIC

ITALIAN, FRENCH, MEXICAN, SPANISH AND CAJUN CUISINE FOR THE HEALTH CONSCIOUS COOK

David & Kathy—
Healthy eating!
Fondly,
Joy

Judy Gilliard & Joy Kirkpatrick, RD

The Guiltless Gourmet Goes Ethnic: Italian, French, Mexican, Spanish and Cajun Cuisine for the Health Conscious Cook
© 1990 by Judy Gilliard and Joy Kirkpatrick, RD.

Library of Congress Cataloging-in-Publication Data

Gilliard, Judy.
   The guiltless gourmet goes ethnic: italian, french, mexican, spanish and cajun cuisine for the health conscious cook.
   /Judy Gilliard & Joy Kirkpatrick.
   p. cm.
   Includes index.
   ISBN 0-937721-68-9 : $11.95
   1. Low-fat diet--Recipes. 2. Salt-free diet--Recipes. 3. Low-calorie diet--Recipes. 4. Cookery, International.
   I. Kirkpatrick, Joy. II. Title.
   RM237.7.G549 1990
   641.5'63--dc20
                                                       90-38818
                                                       CIP
Edited by: Donna Hoel
Illustrations: Teri Gilliard
Photography: William Bartlett, Thoen Photography
Production: Wenda Johnson, Nancy Bolmgren
Printing: Printing Arts, Inc.
Printed in the United States of America

10 9 8 7 6 5 4 3 2 1

Published by:
DCI Publishing
P.O. Box 47945
Mpls, MN 55447-9727

THIS BOOK IS DEDICATED TO OUR FAMILIES, FRIENDS AND CLIENTS WHO ENCOURAGE AND INSPIRE US TO CONTINUE BEING GUILTLESS GOURMETS.

Special acknowledgement to: Bill and Kathy Hanlin and Michael Altenhofen — for legal and business assistance; to Chef Patricia E. Hook, Barbara Sattley, Naomi Guttman and the Food and Nutrition staff at John F. Kennedy Memorial Hospital, Indio, CA, especially Wendy Dunson and to John and Pat Borer — for technical assistance and inspiration. To Bill Kasal for his quick wit and way with words and Neoma Ray for learning her way with figures.

Thanks to our taste testers whose input is invaluable: Pete and Linda Spiers, Ron and Amanda Roisum, Don Mead, George Lanning, Rod Murphy, Tom Virgilio, Marlene and Stewart Schweit, Rose and Walt Edgar, Doug and Susan Edgar, Chuck and Jean Gilliard, Mike Doucette and the staff at KPSI, Mary and Elliot Field, Ric and Rozene Supple, Basil Slaymaker, Larry Johnson, Jan Mazza, Larry Hathaway, Val and Jim Mazza, Re Moreno, Michael and Frank DiPietra, and Ron Barbarita.

Special kudos to Mona Virgilio who spent long hours at the computer and on the phone — a friend and a colleague and to our artist Teri Gilliard for continued clever characterization of THE GUILTLESS GOURMET.

WE SALUTE YOU ONE AND ALL!

Judy and Joy
Spring, 1990

Nutrient analysis done with Diet Wise program from Nutritional Data Resources, Willoughby, Ohio.

Contents

Introduction to Ethnic Cooking
The "Guiltless" Way

Health professionals have been teaching us for years how to reduce our intake of calories, fat, salt, sugar and cholesterol. Many people are becoming expert at modifying everyday recipes, reducing the use of fats and oils and high fat foods. In general, we are becoming more adept at controlling our intake of these items; some have even gained the ability to order in restaurants while remaining true to their healthful diet.

But one delicious area that eludes the health-conscious eater is ethnic foods. No matter which culture we choose to look at, fats and oils, cheeses and sauces, butter and lard are usually major ingredients.

All is not lost! These high-fat ingredients can be greatly reduced and in some cases eliminated without significantly affecting the taste and flavor of the ethnic foods.

We welcome you to *The Guiltless Gourmet Goes Ethnic!* and encourage you to try our lower-fat versions of some of your favorite ethnic foods.

THE GUILTLESS GOURMET GOES ETHNIC

The Pleasure of Your Company

We all must eat to survive. Eating is meant to sustain life. But throughout history eating also has been a social event, a time for gathering with family and friends to share a meal. Good food, good friends and good conversation make for memorable times for all.

Entertaining at home is again on the upsurge. People find it more personal, lending an intimate touch. Parties or gatherings may range from a cozy dinner for two to a brunch for twenty. Still, most of us juggle work and household tasks. This leaves little time to prepare for the much-loved entertaining at home.

Here are a few suggestions on how to make at home entertaining easier.

If the budget allows, hire someone to help serve and do the clean up. This permits you to enjoy your guests, and when the last one leaves, you walk into a clean kitchen!

Form a dinner club. Gather a group of people who like to cook and try new things. Develop a menu and give each person a recipe to make and bring to dinner. This takes all the work away from one person and makes a fun evening.

For those who are just beginning to feel the excitement of entertaining at home, but feel the cost of purchasing different place settings and ornamentation for each type of gathering prohibitive, let us offer these ideas:

Invest in a basic set of plain white dishes. I prefer my serving plates to be 12" buffet plates. They are perfect for any type of dinner motif and they will balance on a lap if need be in a more casual setting.

Now you may build around this set of white dishes with a myriad of different accessories. Choose a few more formal-looking pieces for the center of the table. Select a solid color napkin and tablecloth and the setting becomes formal. A piece of crystal or lucite in the center along with grey, red or peach napkins is all it takes! Don't be limited by these colors. Use your imagination!

When on a trip, pick up unusual pieces for serving or for centerpieces. Perhaps you will find a brightly-colored vase or dried flower arrangement. Use bright, fresh cut flowers laid around a small sombrero and patterned napkins with your basic set of white dishes and you've created a festival!

Have sets of individual vases you can create flower arrangements in. Look for bargains. It doesn't take much to dress up a table and set a mood.

Watch for sales to pick up different colored napkins, tablecloths and place mats.

Another good, small investment for the casual party or afternoon brunch is the basket paper plate holder. These will make inexpensive paper plates look expensive and they're great to have on hand for parties, lunches or snacks.

It doesn't take a lot of money to entertain at home and you'll find the rewards more satisfying. Be creative! Have fun! And, most important, enjoy your company!

Toys For A Fast-Paced Life

They say the older you get the more expensive your toys! So we thought we would suggest some of our favorites. On the top of our list and the most used are:

Food processor in three sizes (large, medium and baby).
    We use the medium the most.
Kitchen Aid Mixer (wire whip, beater and dough hook)
Cordless Mixer (high power)
Crock Pot
Rice Cooker
Bread Baker
Automatic Coffee Maker
Coffee Grinder

We use all of these quite often and laugh at our lifestyles compared with those of grandmothers.

We wonder how they would feel if they could get up in the morning to fresh made coffee and sometimes to a homemade breakfast bread. All we do is put in the dough and set the bread baker to be finished baking at 7 a.m. Voila! Fresh coffee and warm bread await when we arise.

For dinner we might put minestrone soup in the crock pot before leaving for work. We can put ingredients in the bread baker to make a hearty peasant bread and set it to be ready at 6 p.m. During the workday we phone a few friends and invite them over for dinner. Just before they arrive, we toss a salad together and have dinner for six! How easy can it get?

There are other toys we have but don't use as often:

Blender
Espresso Machine
Pasta Machine (We don't recommend this, as it takes
    forever to make and they have such great fresh pasta
    on the market now. But you may feel adventurous and
    enjoy the experience. Don't let us stop you!)
Juicer
Air Popcorn Popper

These and other gadgets are wonderful, but you may prefer the "old fashioned" way. Whatever makes cooking most enjoyable for you is the way you should go!

Tips

Drying Lettuce
Use a salad spinner or lay washed lettuce out on paper towels.

Roasting Peppers
1. Cut tops off pepper, remove seeds, cut in fourths.
2. Place on cookie sheet that has been sprayed with a nonstick cooking spray.
3. Place under broiler until well browned (about 10 min.).
4. Remove skin and cut in strips.

Peeling Tomatoes
1. Remove core of tomato from top. On the bottom of the tomato cut an "X".
2. Drop in a large pan of boiling water for 10 seconds. Remove and place in cold water. The skin will pull right off.

Garlic
Buy garlic in loose heads which are large, firm and tight-skinned. Store in a cool, dry place out of the sun. They will keep up to one month.

Peel Garlic
If you're peeling several cloves, blanch them in boiling water for one minute. Then rinse under cold water and peel.

To peel a few cloves, press each clove with the flat side of a knife until it breaks. Peel skin off.

You can store peeled cloves in olive oil.

Magic of the food processor

Some of our best tips come with the use of the food processor. It also cuts your preparation time in half.

Chopping

Garlic
With steel blade running, drop peeled clove of garlic down feed tube. It will chop to a fine consistency and cling to the sides of your work bowl.

Onions
Peel your onions and cut into fourths. Place in the work bowl with steel blade and make quick on/off pulses with your processor. The onions will cut very quickly. Be careful you don't turn them into mush.

Parsley
Wash and dry parsley. Then place in the work bowl with steel blade. Turn on and run until parsley is all chopped. You can keep fresh chopped parsley in your freezer to use as needed.

Slicing
With your slicing blade, you can slice onions, mushrooms, carrots, celery, cabbage, zucchini, and whatever else you can think of for use in sauces, soups or vegetable dishes.

A mini-food chopper is great for making zest from lemons or oranges. Simply peel the skin from the fruit, cut in pieces and put in chopper. Chop until very fine!

Fresh Lemon Juice/Broths

Squeeze lemons and put juice in ice cube trays. When frozen, pop out and place in plastic bag. It'll be ready in convenient amounts when you need it.

The same thing applies to vegetable broth or chicken broth. By storing it this way, you will not waste any and it'll always be handy.

Spices and Herbs

Spices and herbs are essential to many of our recipes. The fresher the spices, the better. If you're lucky enough to grow your own herbs and spices, you can dry them and store them, or freeze them as mentioned above with parsley.

Remember that, fresh or dried, herbs and spices have a shelf life and will become stale and old. Heat and moisture from your kitchen will even reduce their flavors, so avoid storing them near your range or oven.

Date each new spice or herb purchase with the month and year of purchase. It makes it much easier to keep track of the shelf-life. You may also consider buying them in smaller quantities. This, of course, depends upon how quickly you use a specific spice.

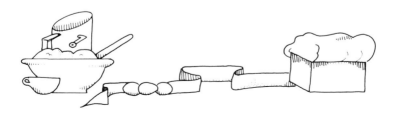

THE GUILTLESS GOURMET GOES ETHNIC

Notes on Ingredients

ALCOHOL: In this book we have used various types of alcohol, vermouth, cognac, wine, tequila and beer. The alcohol calories generally are burned off by heating or cooking with the flavor remaining as well as an insignificant amount of carbohydrate. Alcohol is used in these recipes to add to or enhance the flavor of the recipe. Iit is optional, however, and if you choose to eliminate it as an ingredient, it will not significantly change a recipe.

BEANS: We encourage you to buy dried beans and peas of all varieties. While they may seem bothersome to prepare, they really are not. Soak a pound of beans overnight in a large bowl with plenty of water to cover. Drain and rinse them well the next day and place them in a pot or crock pot with fresh water. Add onion, celery, carrots, chilis, garlic, herbs, whatever flavor you desire. Bring beans to a boil, then reduce to simmer until done. Some beans or peas take only about an hour to cook while others may take four hours or more. When beans are done, cool them slightly, then package them in one- or two-cup portions, label, date and freeze. When a recipe calls for beans, you just pull a package from the freezer. Dried beans and peas are a complex carbohydrate. They have good quality protein, vitamins, minerals and are an excellent source of fiber.

BROTH/BOUILLON: Broths and bouillons are generally very high in sodium content even though they are low in calories. Homemade broth with virtually no salt added is what the calculations in this book are based on for beef or chicken broth. If you choose to use canned broth or bouillon, look for low sodium types, canned or granules.

BUTTER BUDS: Butter Buds™ is the brand name of a fat-free butter flavor substitute that we have found very desirable to work with. It can be used in the dry form or made into a liquid much like melted butter. It is available across the country in grocery stores, usually in the "diet" or "health food" section.

CILANTRO: This pungent herb is used a great deal in Mexican and Southwest cooking. It resembles parsley in appearance but not flavor. Look for it in the fresh produce section of your grocery store or specialty market.

CAPERS: Capers are actually the pickled bud of a low, prickly Mediterranean shrub. They are often used in delicate dishes such as scampi, omelets or as an ingredient in light sauces. Capers are very low in calories, yet high in sodium content — 306 milligrams per tablespoon.

CHEESE: In the following recipes we use a variety of cheeses stressing the lower fat versions as much as possible. Cheese, while being a good source of protein, is also quite high in fat and sodium. Using less cheese and buying low-fat types will allow for plenty of variety.

COCOA: We prefer to use an imported cocoa powder whenever possible. It imparts a much smoother flavor to a recipe. You may find it in your supermarket in the specialty foods area.

CHILIS: There are numerous types and varieties of chilis, many being made available fresh through your produce departments. Chilis range from sweet and mild to very hot. If fresh chilis are available, we encourage you to use them. Ask your produce manager to help you pick out the appropriate variety for the dish you are going to prepare. Fresh chilis should be roasted, peeled and seeded before using. Fresh chilis are very low in calories and usually high in vitamin C. Canned chilis are also low in calories but may contain a higher sodium content depending on how they are packed.

CORN HUSKS: This item is a must for preparing tamales. Dried corn husks are usually available around the fall holidays packaged several dozen per bag. Dried corn husks should be soaked about an hour before using. If you have fresh green corn husks available, these can be used too. Rinse them well and trim them to a workable size.

FRUCTOSE: We chose to use fructose as the primary sweetener for our recipes. We like the taste and texture it imparts. Yet a few words of caution are needed. Fructose is not a sugar substitute — it is crystalized fruit sugar. It is several times sweeter than white sugar (sucrose) so much less is needed to impart a sweet taste. It apparently does not require insulin in order to be used in the body, yet it should not be used in the diet of a diabetic who is not in good control. Check with your doctor or diabetes educator before using fructose in your diet. Fructose can be purchased in a regular grocery store or in a health food store.

JICAMA: A root vegetable also called yam bean, jicama is a low calorie cross between a turnip and a radish in texture and has a mild, crisp and crunchy flavor and texture. Jicama can be found in the fresh produce area of your grocery store. Peel off the heavy brown skin, slice into sticks or chunks to serve with other raw vegetables. Shred jicama into salads or use for making the Jicama Salad (page 139).

MASA: This is a type of corn meal that has been specially ground for making tortillas, tamales and other Mexican and Southwestern style dishes. It can usually be found in your grocery store right next to the regular wheat flour and cornmeal boxes. Store masa and other grain products in the refrigerator or freezer to keep them bug free.

MILK: We recommend nonfat milk or 1% milk for all of our recipes. If preferred, nonfat will work for all of them, but we find 1% milk provides extra flavor and texture without adding significantly to the fat calories in a recipe.

SALT OR SODIUM: None of the recipes in this book have added salt. If you don't need to restrict salt intake, you are free to add salt to taste. Some of the ingredients we use will have a higher sodium content, i.e., capers, and certain types of canned tomatoes. However, we leave the decision up to you as to whether you want to add salt or not. The sodium content per serving is listed for every recipe in this book.

TOMATOES: We use tomatoes in many of the recipes in this book. In some cases the low-salt or no-salt-added types are preferred if available in your area. For various recipes where a particular cut or texture of tomato is important, the regular canned varieties are used. These will run higher in sodium. The sodium content of each serving of a recipe is listed in this book.

TORTILLAS: Tortillas come in two basic types — corn and flour. Corn tortillas, store bought or homemade, are made without added fat while flour tortillas generally are made with lard, vegetable shortening or oil. Tortillas come in different sizes as well — flour tortillas often equal two corn tortillas in size and calories. We use standard-sized corn tortillas for our recipes and use our own recipe for flour tortillas, which are made more to size with corn tortillas.

Section I
Italian

Italian

The Italian cuisine adapts easily to a low-fat, high-complex carbohydrate diet. You will always find the Italian kitchen warm and friendly as Italians look upon cooking as a pleasure. They take their food seriously, but also feel there should be fun in both cooking and eating.

Italian foods are prepared simply with simple ingredients. Pasta is served at almost every meal, and the freshest of ingredients are always used.

Use fresh herbs whenever possible. When buying dried herbs, buy them in small quantities and keep them in air-tight containers in a cool place. One part dried herbs is equivalent to three parts fresh.

Olive oil is considered one of the healthiest oils for you. The best to buy is extra virgin, which is made from the first cold pressing. It has a very delicate flavor and is suitable for all recipes here. It's more expensive than other oil, but it's worth it. And since we use very little oil in our recipes, it will last a long time. You can keep olive oil for up to one year in a cool, dark place. You may want to decant it in a small ceramic or glass container for handy use. (Don't use plastic as it will change the flavor.)

Italian Dinner Party

The family style dinner
If you have ever been to an Italian home for dinner
on a Sunday night,
you will remember the food keeps coming and coming.
Here is a suggested
menu to treat your friends.

Appetizer Salad
Antipasto

Soup
Minestrone

Pasta
Linguini with Clam Sauce

Main Course
Chicken with Lemon and Capers
Risotto

Dessert
Almond Yogurt Cake
Expresso

Informal Italian Supper

Tomato and Cucumber Salad

Pasta and Bean Soup

Bread Sticks

Bowl of Fresh Fruit

Planning Ahead With Italian Cuisine

It seems that quite a few items intermingle well with Italian cuisine, so we chose quite a few recipes which do just that. Here is a list of items that are handy to make ahead and keep in your freezer. Be sure to label items with the item, the amount, and the date you made it. Rotate your items so one thing doesn't get stuck in the back of your freezer for a year! Items are best if used within three to six months. Freeze in different sizes depending on the size of your family.

Marinara Sauce (page 41)
Mushroom Sauce (page 40)
Meat Sauce (page 42)
Manicotti Filling (page 48)
Zucchini Filling (page 47)
Fresh chopped parsley (see Tips)

Minestrone

1   pound dry beans
1   tablespoon olive oil
1   medium onion, chopped
1   clove garlic, chopped
1   teaspoon oregano
1   teaspoon basil
1 1/2   cups celery, sliced 1/4 inch
2   cups carrots, chopped
2   cups zucchini, sliced 1/4 inch
1   cup cabbage, sliced thin
1   pound mushrooms, washed and sliced
2   28 oz. canned, diced tomatoes in juice
6   cups water
2   beef bouillon cubes, low sodium preferred
1/2   pound elbow macaroni, cooked
1/2   cup fresh parsley, chopped

1. Soak beans overnight. Rinse.
2. Heat olive oil in large Dutch oven. Add onion and garlic and saute until soft. Add oregano and basil. Saute 30 seconds.
3. Add celery, carrots, zucchini, cabbage, mushrooms, tomatoes in juice, water, bouillon cubes. Bring to simmer.
4. Simmer 2 to 3 hours until beans are tender.
5. Add cooked macaroni and parsley.

This can be made in a crock pot at step #4. Put all ingredients in crock pot. Cook on high all day. Add pasta and parsley right before serving.

Makes 8 servings.

Each serving contains:
328   calories
17   grams protein
61   grams carbohydrate
4   grams fat

100 mg. sodium
0 mg. cholesterol
11 grams fiber

ADA Exchange Value
4 Starch
$^1/_2$ Fat
10% of total calories are from fat.

Pasta and Bean Soup

1 *pound small white beans*
1 *tablespoon olive oil*
1 *clove garlic, minced*
1 *medium onion, chopped*
1 *teaspoon Italian seasoning*
2 *tablespoons fresh, chopped parsley*
2 *celery stalks, chopped*
2 *medium carrots, sliced ¼ inch rounds*
3 *rosemary leaves, chopped*
5 *cups Chicken Broth (page 124)*
1 *can diced tomatoes with juice*
 black pepper to taste
½ *pound cooked pasta shells*

1. Soak beans overnight. Rinse.
2. In a large Dutch oven, heat olive oil. Saute onion and garlic until soft. Add Italian seasoning and chopped parsley. Saute 30 seconds.
3. Add celery, carrots, rosemary, Chicken Broth, diced tomatoes with juice and pepper. Heat to simmer.
4. Add beans. Cover and simmer 2 to 3 hours until beans are tender.
5. Add cooked pasta and serve.

This can be made in the crock pot at step #4. Put all ingredients in the crock pot and cook all day on high, adding pasta right before serving.

Makes 10 servings.

Each serving contains:
 236 *calories*
 12 *grams protein*
 43 *grams carbohydrate*
 3 *grams fat*

628 mg. sodium
   negligible mg. cholesterol
  6 grams fiber

  ADA Exchange Value
  2 Starch
  1 Vegetable
  1 Lean Meat
10% of total calories are from fat.

Vinaigrette Dressing

1/4 **cup olive oil**
1/2 **teaspoon garlic powder**
2 **teaspoons Worcestershire Sauce**
1 **teaspoon dry mustard**
dash **Tabasco sauce**
1/2 **teaspoon ground black pepper**
   juice from 1/2 lemon
1 **cup wine vinegar (red or white)**
1 **cup water**

1. Combine all ingredients in a blender or covered container and mix well.
2. Store in a covered container. Chill.
3. Makes 2 cups.

Makes 16 servings. 1 serving = 2 tablespoons.

Each serving contains:
   33   calories
        negligible grams protein
   1   gram carbohydrate
   3   grams fat
   11   mg. sodium
   0   mg. cholesterol
        negligible grams fiber

   ADA Exchange Value
   1   Fat
   82%   of total calories are from fat.

Variations of Vinaigrette used in other recipes

Caesar Dressing

$^1/_2$ *cup Vinaigrette Dressing*
1 *egg, coddled*
2 *tablespoons Parmesan cheese, grated*

Combine ingredients and chill.

Makes 4 servings.

Each serving contains:
  98 *calories*
   3 *grams protein*
   3 *grams carbohydrate*
   9 *grams fat*
  86 *mg. sodium*
  71 *mg. cholesterol*
     negligible grams fiber

     ADA Exchange Value
   1 *Vegetable*
   2 *Fat*
83% *of total calories are from fat*

Basil Dressing

$^1/_2$ **cup Vinaigrette Dressing**
$^1/_2$ **teaspoons basil (crushed with mortar and pestle)**

Combine ingredients and chill.

Makes 4 servings.

Each serving contains:
     67 *calories*
          negligible grams protein
      2 *grams carbohydrate*
      7 *grams fat*
    22 *mg. sodium*
      0 *mg. cholesterol*
          negligible grams fiber

          ADA Exchange Value
      1 *Fat*
  95% *of total calories are from fat.*

Antipasto Dressing

Also an excellent marinade for beef, lamb or chicken.

 2 *tablespoons olive oil*
 3 *garlic cloves, minced*
 1/4 *cup lemon juice*
 1/2 *teaspoon cilantro (coriander)*
 2 *teaspoons oregano*
 2/3 *cup white wine vinegar*
 dash *cayenne pepper*

1. Combine all ingredients in a blender or covered container and blend well.
2. Store in a covered container and chill.
3. Makes 1 cup.

Makes 8 servings. 1 serving = 2 tablespoons

Each serving contains:
 37 *calories*
   negligible grams protein
 2 *grams carbohydrate*
 4 *grams fat*
 2 *mg. sodium*
 0 *mg. cholesterol*
 0 *grams fiber*

   ADA Exchange Value
 1 *Fat*
 85% *of total calories are from fat.*

Caesar Salad

1 *large head romaine lettuce*
$^1/_2$ *cup Caesar Salad Dressing (page 30)*
1 *cup Crunchy Croutons (page 35)*
2 *tablespoons Parmesan cheese, freshly grated*

1. Wash romaine lettuce well. Drain and tear into bite-sized pieces. Spin or pat dry.
2. Add dressing and toss well.
3. Add croutons and toss lightly.
4. Place on four salad plates and sprinkle each with $^1/_2$ tablespoon Parmesan cheese.

Makes 4 servings.

Each serving contains:
        139 calories
          6 grams protein
          7 grams carbohydrate
        10 grams fat
      189 mg. sodium
        73 mg. cholesterol
          2 grams fiber

          ADA Exchange Value
          1 Vegetable
        $^1/_4$ Starch
          2 Fat
      63% of total calories are from fat.

Antipasto Salad

9 ounce package frozen artichoke hearts (steam 2 minutes)
2 cups green beans, cut into 3 inch pieces (steam 5 minutes)
1 green or red sweet pepper, sliced (steam 2 minutes)
1 cucumber, cut in half lengthwise, seed and slice
$1/4$ pound fresh mushrooms, sliced
$1/2$ cup Antipasto Salad Dressing (page 32)

Toss all ingredients. Cover and chill for several hours, stirring occasionally.

Makes 4 generous servings.

Each serving contains:
82 calories
3 grams protein
12 grams carbohydrate
4 grams fat
28 mg. sodium
0 mg. cholesterol
4 grams fiber

ADA Exchange Value
2 Vegetables
$1/2$ Fat
43% of total calories are from fat.

Crunchy Croutons

Ever wonder what to do with those last few slices of bread in the loaf that somehow become wrinkled, stiff or dry? Well, as a great money saver and tasty topping maker, with a few extra minutes, these dry bread slices can be converted into Crunchy Croutons. Store them in your "pantry" in an airtight plastic container with a tight fitting lid.

> **2 slices dry, whole grain bread**
> **garlic powder, basil and/or oregano to taste**

1. Preheat oven to 250 degrees.
2. Cut bread into small cubes and place on a nonstick cookie sheet.
3. Sprinkle lightly with garlic powder, basil and/or oregano to taste.
4. Bake until lightly browned and crunchy, about 10 to 15 minutes.

Makes 4 servings. 1 serving = $1/4$ cup

Each serving contains:
- **28 calories**
- **1 gram protein**
- **6 grams carbohydrate**
- **negligible grams fat**
- **61 mg. sodium**
- **negligible mg. cholesterol**
- **1 gram fiber**

ADA Exchange Value
$1/2$ Starch
negligible fat calories.

Basic Dough
for Pizza and Bread Sticks

Makes 2 15-inch pizzas, or 6 calzones, or 12 baby calzones, or 12 long bread sticks, or 24 short bread sticks.

This recipe calls for part corn meal. We like it because it makes the dough a little crisper and adds a bit more texture. For a change you could omit the corn meal or replace it with unbleached or whole wheat flour.

> 1 **package dry yeast**
> 1/4 **cup warm water**
> 1/4 **teaspoon fructose**
> 1 **cup cold milk**
> 1 **tablespoon olive oil**
> 2 1/2 **cups unbleached flour**
> 1/2 **cup corn meal**
> 1/2 **teaspoon salt**

1. Mix yeast, water and fructose in a measuring cup and let set for 5 minutes to proof.
2. Add milk to the yeast mixture.
3. Place flour, corn meal and salt in food processor with plastic blade.
4. Turn on machine and process in the yeast mixture. Then add the oil slowly. Dough should be very soft. If not, add more milk, a drop at a time.
5. Let the dough rest 5 minutes. Then process 5 seconds.
6. Turn the dough out on a lightly floured work surface.
7. Knead 50 strokes by hand. Let rest 5 minutes. Then knead 20 more times to make a soft, smooth dough.
8. Place dough into a bowl. Cover with a cloth and let rise 1 1/2 hours, until double in bulk.
9. Take out dough and cut into portions. You can refrigerate or freeze the dough for later, but it must be brought back to room temperature.

Makes 8 servings of pizza dough.

Each serving contains:
- *190 calories*
- *6 grams protein*
- *36 grams carbohydrate*
- *2 grams fat*
- *154 mg. sodium*
- *negligible mg. cholesterol*
- *1 gram fiber*

ADA Exchange Value
- *2 Starch*
- *½ Fat*
- *10% of total calories are from fat.*

Makes 16 servings of bread sticks.

Each serving contains:
- *95 calories*
- *3 grams protein*
- *18 grams carbohydrate*
- *1 gram fat*
- *77 mg. sodium*
- *negligible mg. cholesterol*
- *negligible grams fiber*

ADA Exchange Value
- *1 Starch*
- *10% of total calories are from fat.*

Pizza and/or Calzones

Oh, boy, you can have some fun with this one. Almost anything can go on top of a pizza. How about a pizza party? Make the pizza dough and the tomato sauce and ask each one of your guests to bring one low-fat topping. You can even have a dessert pizza!

Mushroom and Cheese Pizza

Pizza dough for one pizza (page 36)
1 *cup Marinara Sauce (page 41)*
1 *cup sliced mushrooms*
¹/₂ *cup grated mozzarella cheese*
¹/₂ *teaspoon Italian seasoning*

1. Preheat oven to 450 degrees.
2. Roll out dough on a lightly floured board in a circle ¹/₄ inch thick. Place on a round pizza pan and press out with hand to fit.
3. Cover with Marinara Sauce, then sliced mushrooms, then mozzarella cheese. Finally, sprinkle evenly with Italian seasoning.
4. Bake 7 to 10 minutes until edges have puffed up and the cheese is melted.

Cut in 6 pieces. Makes 3 servings.

Variations

Add:

¹/₂ *cup cooked Italian sausage or*
¹/₂ *cup cooked ground turkey or*
¹/₄ *cup grated pepperoni or*
thinly sliced onion and bell pepper or
all of the above!

To turn your pizza into a calzone, just fold it in half and pinch the edges together. Bake until brown (15 minutes).

Each serving contains:

- *300 calories*
- *13 grams protein*
- *43 grams carbohydrate*
- *9 grams fat*
- *510 mg sodium*
- *23 mg. cholesterol*
- *4 grams fiber*

ADA Exchange Value

- *2 starch*
- *2 vegetable*
- *1 med. fat meat*
- *1 fat*
- *27% of total calories from fat.*

Mushroom Sauce

1   tablespoon olive oil
2   cloves garlic, chopped
1   medium onion, chopped
1   teaspoon basil
$^1/_2$ teaspoon oregano
$^1/_2$ teaspoon ground red pepper
1   pound mushrooms, sliced
1   28 oz. can diced tomatoes in juice
1   28 oz. can whole Italian plum tomatoes with basil
1   28 oz. can tomato puree
1   28 oz. can tomato sauce
1   tablespoon fresh chopped parsley

1. Heat olive oil in large Dutch oven. Add garlic and onion.
   Saute until soft.
2. Add basil, oregano and red pepper. Saute 30 seconds.
3. Add mushrooms. Saute until tender and most of the liquid is
   absorbed.
4. Add all the cans of tomatoes and fresh parsley. Simmer for 1
   hour.

Makes 12 cups. Makes 12 servings.

Each serving contains:

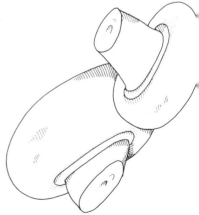

80   calories
3   grams protein
16   grams carbohydrate
2   grams fat
559   mg. sodium
0   mg. cholesterol
6   grams fiber

ADA Exchange Value
3   Vegetables
21%   of total calories from fat.

Basic Marinara Sauce

1 tablespoon olive oil
2 cloves garlic, chopped
1 medium onion, sliced
1 teaspoon Italian seasoning
2 28 oz. can diced tomatoes in juice
1 28 oz. can tomato puree
2 tablespoons fresh parsley, chopped

1. Heat olive oil in large Dutch oven. Add garlic and onion. Saute until tender.
2. Add Italian seasoning. Cook 30 seconds.
3. Add diced tomatoes with juice, tomato puree and parsley. Stir.
4. Turn heat to low and simmer for 1 hour.

Makes 8 1/2 cups. Makes 10 servings.

Each serving contains:
80 *calories*
3 *grams protein*
15 *grams carbohydrate*
2 *grams fat*
797 *mg. sodium*
0 *mg. cholesterol*
6 *grams fiber*

ADA Exchange Value
2 *Vegetable*
1/2 *Fat*
23% *of total calories are from fat.*

Meat Sauce

1 tablespoon olive oil
1 medium onion, chopped
1 clove garlic, minced
2 medium carrots, chopped
1 medium green pepper, chopped
1 teaspoon Italian seasoning
2 tablespoons fresh parsley, chopped
1 28 oz. can diced tomatoes in juice
1 28 oz. can tomato sauce
1 pound extra lean ground beef
1 bay leaf

1. In a large Dutch oven, heat olive oil. Saute onion, garlic, carrots and green pepper until soft.
2. Add Italian seasoning and saute 30 seconds. Add parsley.
3. In a nonstick skillet, saute ground beef until done. Drain on paper towels to remove excess fat.
4. Add beef to Dutch oven. Add tomatoes in juice and tomato sauce and bring to a simmer. Add bay leaf. Cover and simmer 2 hours.

Makes 7 cups. Makes 10 servings.

Each serving contains:
  142 *calories*
   13 *grams protein*
   13 *grams carbohydrate*
    5 *grams fat*
  685 *mg. sodium*
   29 *mg. cholesterol*
    5 *grams fiber*

      ADA Exchange Value
    2 *Vegetable*
 1 ¹/₂ *Medium Fat Meat*
  31% *of total calories are from fat.*

Meatballs Marinara

$1/2$ pound very lean ground beef
1 egg white
$1/2$ teaspoon garlic powder
$1/4$ teaspoon black pepper
2 teaspoons parsley, freshly chopped
1 tablespoon parmesan cheese
$1/4$ cup Crunchy Croutons (page 35)
2 cups Basic Marinara Sauce (page 41)

1. Mix all ingredients except Marinara Sauce in a bowl.
2. Form into 16 walnut-sized meatballs.
3. Brown meatballs on all sides in a nonstick pan sprayed with a nonstick spray.
4. Add Marinara Sauce. Cover and simmer for 30 minutes.

Makes 4 servings.

Each serving contains:
148 calories
16 grams protein
10 grams carbohydrate
5 grams fat
509 mg. sodium
37 mg. cholesterol
3 grams fiber

ADA Exchange Value
$1 1/2$ Lean Meat
2 Vegetable
32% of total calories are from fat.

Rolled Eggplant

 2 medium eggplants, sliced lengthwise $^1/_4$ inch
    (8 slices — don't use ends)
1 $^1/_2$ cups Zucchini Filling (page 47)
 3 cups Marinara Sauce (page 41)
 2 cups low-fat cottage cheese
$^1/_2$ teaspoon ground garlic
 2 tablespoons grated Parmesan cheese
 2 teaspoons fresh parsley, chopped
$^1/_4$ cup sliced ripe olives

1. On a cookie sheet sprayed with a nonstick spray, bake eggplant at 350 degrees for 10 minutes.
2. Place a large spoonful of zucchini filling in each slice of eggplant and roll up. Place seam side down in a bake-and-serve dish, making two rolls per serving.
3. Spoon Marinara Sauce down center of each roll.
4. Place cottage cheese in food processor or blender with garlic and Parmesan cheese and blend until smooth and creamy.
5. Spoon cottage cheese down center of each roll. Sprinkle parsley down center of that. Place olives down center of that. Your end result should be very pretty and rolls of different colors.

Makes 4 servings.

Each serving contains:
   249 *calories*
    21 *grams protein*
    27 *grams carbohydrate*
     8 *grams fat*
  1290 *mg. sodium*
    12 *mg. cholesterol*
     9 *grams fiber*

         ADA Exchange Value
     3 *Lean Meat*
     2 *Vegetable*
   30% *of total calories are from fat.*

Ratatouille

Servings are large and chocked full of low calorie vegetables.

> 1 *large onion, sliced*
> 4 *medium zucchini, sliced*
> 1 *green or red sweet pepper, seeded and sliced*
> 1 *eggplant, peeled and cubed*
> 4 *tomatoes, chopped in large pieces*
> $1/4$ *cup tomato paste*
> $1/2$ *teaspoon minced garlic*
> $1/4$ *cup fresh parsley, chopped*
> 2 *teaspoons sweet basil*
> 1 *teaspoon oregano*
> $1/4$ *teaspoon black pepper*

1. Combine all ingredients in a large saucepan.
2. Cook over medium heat until all vegetables are tender, stirring frequently.
3. Reduce heat, cover and simmer 10 to 15 minutes.
4. Remove cover and continue cooking until liquid has evaporated and mixture has thickened.
5. May be served hot or cold.

Makes 6 servings.

Each serving contains:
> 54 *calories*
> 2 *grams protein*
> 12 *grams carbohydrate*
> *negligible grams fat*
> 17 *mg. sodium*
> 0 *mg. cholesterol*
> 4 *grams fiber*
>
> *ADA Exchange Value*
> 2 *Vegetable*
> *negligible fat calories.*

Eggplant, Pepper, Tomatoes and Ziti

1 tablespoon olive oil
2 cloves garlic
1 pound eggplant peeled and cut in $1/2$ inch cubes
2 teaspoons capers
2 large red or yellow peppers cut in half then in $1/4$ inch strips
1 28 oz. can diced tomatoes in juice
2 thinly sliced fresh basil
  ground black pepper to taste
1 pound ziti
$1/3$ cup grated parmesan

1. Heat oil in skillet. Add garlic and saute until golden brown. Remove garlic and discard.
2. Add eggplant and saute until soft.
3. Add peppers, capers, tomatoes with juice, basil and pepper. Bring to simmer. Cover and cook 30 minutes, stirring occasionally.
4. Cook pasta and drain.
5. Add sauce to pasta and toss with parmesan cheese.

Makes 6 servings.

Each serving contains:
223 *calories*
7 *grams protein*
43 *grams carbohydrate*
3 *grams fat*
435 *mg. sodium*
0 *mg. cholesterol*
5 *grams fiber*

ADA Exchange Value
2 *Starch*
1 *Vegetable*
1 *Fat*
14% *of total calories are from fat.*

Zucchini Filling

This is an all around great filling that is very low in calories!

1 tablespoon olive oil
1 clove garlic, chopped
2 medium onions, chopped
$^1/_2$ teaspoon basil
$^1/_2$ teaspoon oregano
$^1/_4$ teaspoon ground red chili pepper
1 green pepper, chopped
2 pounds zucchini, sliced $^1/_4$ inch
1 pound mushrooms, sliced
1 28 oz. can diced tomatoes in juice

1. In a Dutch oven, heat oil. Add onions and garlic. Saute until tender. Add herbs and saute 30 seconds.
2. Add remaining ingredients. Cover and simmer 15 minutes.
3. Uncover and cook on medium heat until liquid is reduced.

Makes 6 cups. Makes 8 servings.

Each serving contains:
71 calories
3 grams protein
12 grams carbohydrate
3 grams fat
174 mg. sodium
0 mg. cholesterol
4 grams fiber

ADA Exchange Value
2 Vegetable
$^1/_2$ Fat
32% of total calories are from fat.

Manicotti

12 *manicotti shells cooked al dente*
1 *tablespoon olive oil*
1 *medium onion, chopped*
1 *garlic clove, minced*
1 *10 oz. package chopped, frozen spinach,*
 cooked, drained and squeezed dry
1 *pound skimmed ricotta cheese*
1 *pound mushrooms, sliced and cooked*
1 *cup grated mozzarella cheese*
1 *teaspoon Italian seasoning*
3 *cups Marinara Sauce (page 41)*

1. Heat olive oil in skillet. Add onion and garlic and saute until soft.
2. Mix all ingredients in a bowl, including onion and garlic.
3. Divide into 12 portions and fill each manicotti shell with one portion.
4. Line filled shell in a serving dish you can bake in. Spoon Marinara Sauce over the top. Cover and bake at 350 degrees 45 minutes.

Makes 6 servings.

Each serving contains:
  313 *calories*
   18 *grams protein*
   36 *grams carbohydrate*
   12 *grams fat*
  627 *mg. sodium*
   52 *mg. cholesterol*
    6 *grams fiber*

  ADA Exchange Value
    2 *Starch*
    1 *Vegetable*
    2 *Medium Fat Meat*
  35% *of total calories are from fat.*

Linguini With Clam Sauce

15 ounces diced tomatoes in juice
1 6 1/2 ounce can chopped clams
1 clove garlic, minced
2 tablespoons capers
3 tablespoons fresh parsley, chopped
1 teaspoon olive oil
1/2 teaspoon freshly ground black pepper
1/2 pound cooked and drained pasta

1. Heat olive oil in a large nonstick skillet.
2. Saute garlic and capers for 1 minute.
3. Add tomatoes, parsley, pepper and clams. Simmer for 5 minutes uncovered.
4. Toss with pasta and serve.

Makes 4 servings.

Each serving contains:
139 calories
11 grams protein
18 grams carbohydrate
3 grams fat
244 mg. sodium
38 mg. cholesterol
1 gram fiber

ADA Exchange Value
1 Starch
1/2 Fat
1/2 Lean Meat
17% of total calories are from fat.

Lasagne

1 **pound lasagne noodles**
6 **cups Meat Sauce (page 42)**
2 **cups Zucchini Filling (page 47)**
2 **cups low-fat cottage cheese, blended in blender or food processor until smooth**
$^1/_3$ **cup grated Parmesan cheese**
1 **cup grated mozzarella cheese**

1. Cook lasagne noodles in large pot of boiling water until slightly underdone. Drain and rinse in cold water.
2. Spray lasagne pan well with a nonstick spray.
3. Put a layer of noodles in pan. Top with 4 cups of Meat Sauce. Top that with cottage cheese. Sprinkle with Parmesan cheese. Top with another layer of noodles. Spread the Zucchini Filling over them. Top with the remaining noodles. Spread the remaining 2 cups of Meat Sauce next. Sprinkle the mozzarella cheese over the top.
4. Cover pan and bake in a 350 degree oven 45 minutes. Let stand 10 minutes before cutting.

Makes 10 servings.

Each serving contains:
409 *calories*
30 *grams protein*
47 *grams carbohydrate*
12 *grams fat*
965 *mg. sodium*
83 *mg. cholesterol*
6 *grams fiber*

ADA Exchange Value
2 *Starch*
3 *Medium Fat Meat*
2 *Vegetable*
26% *of calories are from fat.*

Pasta Primavera

$^1/_2$ cup carrots, grated
1 cup zucchini, grated or diced
3 large green onions, diced, green part only
$^1/_2$ teaspoon minced garlic
1 cup broccoli flowerettes (steam 3 to 5 minutes)
$^1/_2$ cup small peas (steam 3 to 5 minutes)
1 tablespoon chopped parsley
$^1/_2$ teaspoon Italian seasoning
1 cup nonfat milk
2 teaspoons cornstarch
1 tablespoon liquid Butter Buds™
$^1/_4$ cup low fat sour cream
$^1/_2$ cup grated parmesan cheese
   pepper to taste
4 cups cooked pasta

1. Spray a large skillet with a nonstick coating. Saute carrots, zucchini, onions and garlic until tender.
2. Add cornstarch to milk and mix until dissolved.
3. Add liquid Butter Buds™ to milk.
4. Stir milk mixture into sauteed vegetables. Stir over medium heat until sauce thickens.
5. Stir in sour cream, parsley and seasoning.
6. Add broccoli and peas. Stir in gently.
7. Place pasta that has been well drained in a bowl.
8. Pour sauce over pasta. Add parmesan cheese and toss thoroughly.
9. Serve immediately.

Makes 4 servings.

Each serving contains:
- 310   *calories*
- 15   *grams protein*
- 47   *grams carbohydrate*
- 7   *grams fat*
- 230   *mg. sodium*
- 11   *mg. cholesterol*
- 5   *grams fiber*

ADA Exchange Value
- 3   *Starch*
- 1   *Vegetable*
- 1   *Medium Fat Meat*
- 21%   *of total calories are from fat.*

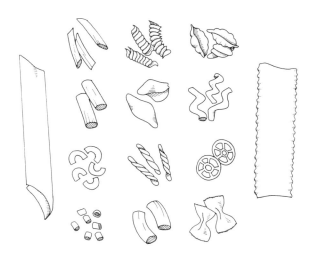

Lasagne Roll-Ups

This is a fun way to make lasagne. It can look a bit more formal for a dinner party and also is a great way to make it for individual freezing for a quick meal when there is no time to cook! Like pizza, there is a never ending way to make a roll-up.

Meat Sauce Roll-Ups

1   pound lasagne noodles (16 noodles)
Meat Sauce recipe (page 42)
8   oz. mozzarella cheese, grated

1. In a large pot, cook noodles (slightly undercook). Drain and rinse.
2. Lay out each noodle. Put 1/3 cup sauce down the center of each and roll up. Place 2 rolls in individual bake-and-serve dishes. Top with 1/3 cup sauce and 1 oz. cheese. (Or you can line them up in a large bake-and-serve dish.)
3. Bake covered at 350 degrees for 30 minutes.

Makes 8 servings.

Each serving contains:

457	*calories*
28	*grams protein*
55	*grams carbohydrate*
15	*grams fat*
965	*mg. sodium*
108	*mg. cholesterol*
8	*grams fiber*

ADA Exchange Value

3	*Starch*
2	*Vegetable*
2	*Medium Fat Meat*
1	*Fat*
29%	*of total calories are from fat.*

Ricotta Spinach Roll-Up

1 **pound lasagne noodles**
1 **recipe Manicotti Filling (page 48)**
4 **cups Marinara Sauce (page 41)**

Prepare the same as Lasagne Roll-Ups except use $1/16$ of the Manicotti Filling for each noodle and top each roll with $1/4$ cup Marinara Sauce.

Makes 8 servings.

Each serving contains:
- 407 *calories*
- 20 *grams protein*
- 60 *grams carbohydrate*
- 12 *grams fat*
- 908 *mg. sodium*
- 71 *mg. cholesterol*
- 9 *grams fiber*

  ADA Exchange Value
- 3 *Starch*
- 2 *Vegetable*
- 1 *Medium Fat Meat*
- 1 *Fat*
- 26% *of total calories are from fat.*

Scampi

1 tablespoon olive oil
2 cloves garlic, minced
1 medium onion, chopped
1 green pepper, chopped
1/4 teaspoon ground red chili pepper
1/2 cup dry vermouth
1 15 oz. can diced tomatoes, drained
1 pound raw shrimp, shell removed and cleaned

1. Heat oil in a large skillet. Add onion, garlic and green pepper. Saute until tender.
2. Add ground red pepper and vermouth. Cook until liquid is almost all absorbed.
3. Add tomatoes. Cook on medium until hot, almost to a boil.
4. Add shrimp and cook until done (about 3 minutes).

Makes 4 servings.

Each serving contains:
202 *calories*
27 *grams protein*
8 *grams carbohydrate*
6 *grams fat*
207 *mg. sodium*
200 *mg. cholesterol*
2 *grams fiber*

ADA Exchange Value
3 *Lean Meat*
1 *Vegetable*
1 *Fat*
27% *of total calories are from fat.*

Halibut Cacciatore

1 *green bell pepper, sliced*
3 *cups Mushroom Sauce (page 40)*
1 *pound halibut (in 12 pieces)*

1. In a large skillet sprayed with a nonstick spray, saute green pepper until soft.
2. Add Mushroom Sauce. Bring to simmer. Add the halibut. Cover and simmer 20 minutes or until halibut is cooked.

Makes 6 servings.

Each serving contains:
- 150 *calories*
- 22 *grams protein*
- 9 *grams carbohydrate*
- 3 *grams fat*
- 333 *mg. sodium*
- 32 *mg. cholesterol*
- 3 *grams fiber*

ADA Exchange Value
- 3 *Lean Meat*
- 1 *Vegetable*
- 19% *of total calories are from fat.*

Chicken Cacciatore

1 tablespoon olive oil
6 4 oz. chicken breasts, skin removed
1 medium onion, sliced
2 cloves garlic, minced
1 teaspoon oregano
1 pound mushrooms, sliced
1 28 oz. can diced tomatoes in juice
1 28 oz. can tomato sauce
1/2 teaspoon black pepper
2 tablespoons fresh parsley, chopped
1 bell pepper
1 pound pasta

1. Heat olive oil in Dutch oven.
2. Brown chicken breast and remove from pan.
3. Add onion and garlic and saute until soft. Add oregano and saute 30 seconds.
4. Add mushrooms and bell pepper. Cover and simmer 5 minutes. Uncover and cook until liquid is reduced.
5. Add tomatoes, tomato sauce, pepper and parsley. Bring to simmer.
6. Add chicken breasts, cover and simmer 45 minutes.

Makes 6 servings.

Each serving contains:

420 calories
41 grams protein
47 grams carbohydrate
8 grams fat
681 mg. sodium
88 mg. cholesterol
7 grams fiber

ADA Exchange Value
4 Lean Meat
2 Vegetable
2 Starch
17% of total calories are from fat.

THE GUILTLESS GOURMET GOES ETHNIC

Italian Eggs

3/4 **cup chicken broth**
2 **cups mushrooms, sliced**
1 **medium onion, sliced**
1 **bell pepper, sliced**
1/2 **teaspoon Italian seasoning**
  dash crushed hot red pepper
4 **small to medium red potatoes, cooked and sliced in large pieces**
3 **whole eggs**
3 **egg whites**

1. Reduce 1/2 cup broth to 1 tablespoon in a nonstick skillet.
2. Saute mushrooms and set aside.
3. Reduce 1/4 cup broth to 1 tablespoon and saute onion and bell pepper until tender.
4. Add seasonings, potatoes and mushrooms. Toss until warm.
5. Beat eggs and egg whites together. Add to vegetables, stirring until set.

Makes 4 servings.

Each serving contains:
214 **calories**
11 **grams protein**
33 **grams carbohydrate**
5 **grams fat**
354 **mg. sodium**
206 **mg. cholesterol**
4 **grams fiber**

ADA Exchange Value
2 **Starch/Bread**
1/2 **Lean Meat**
1/2 **Fat**
20% **of total calories are from fat.**

Risotto

Risotto is the Italian version of rice and can be made in many variations — from a side dish to a main course. The traditional way is to brown the rice and keep adding liquid until it is absorbed and the rice is cooked. We have kept part of the tradition but have made it a bit easier and healthier.

The rice used is Italy Arborio, a hard grain rice which is quite good. You can use either that or a brown rice in these recipes. If you have a rice cooker, you can put the ingredients in it after you have completed the sauteing steps. It works perfectly and will keep the rice warm until you are ready to serve it.

Plain Risotto

> 2 *tablespoons margarine*
> 1 *medium onion, chopped*
> 1 *cup brown rice*
> ¹/₄ *cup grated parmesan cheese*
> 2 *cups Chicken Broth (page 124)*

1. In a sauce pan, melt margarine on medium high heat.
2. Add onion and saute until soft. Add rice and saute until all rice is coated.
3. Add cheese and chicken broth. Bring to a boil, then simmer. Cover and cook until all liquid is absorbed.

Makes 4 servings.

Each serving contains:
> 124 *calories*
> 4 *grams protein*
> 15 *grams carbohydrate*
> 5 *grams fat*
> 942 *mg. sodium*
> 5 *mg. cholesterol*
> 1 *gram fiber*

> *ADA Exchange Value*
> 1 *Starch*
> 1 *Fat*
> 36% *of total calories are from fat.*

Lemon Cheese Pie

Crust:

2 teaspoons corn oil margarine
4 graham cracker squares
$^1/_2$ teaspoon allspice
$^1/_2$ teaspoon lemon peel

Filling:

2 cups lowfat cottage cheese
$^1/_4$ cup fructose
2 teaspoons vanilla
1 teaspoon lemon peel
1 teaspoon fresh lemon juice

Topping:

$^3/_4$ cup low-fat sour cream
2 tablespoons fructose
1 $^1/_2$ teaspoons vanilla

1. Preheat oven to 375 degrees.
2. Put graham crackers, allspice and lemon peel in a food processor or blender and blend into crumbs.
3. Melt margarine and slowly pour into the graham cracker crumbs while blender is running.
4. Place crumbs in a 9 inch pie plate that has been sprayed with a nonstick spray, and press down evenly with finger tips.
5. Put cottage cheese, fructose, vanilla, lemon peel and lemon juice in a food processor or blender and blend until smooth.
6. Pour cottage cheese mixture into the graham cracker shell.
7. Bake for 15 minutes.
8. While pie is baking, combine topping ingredients in a mixing bowl and mix thoroughly.
9. Remove pie from oven and spread topping evenly over the top.
10. Place back in the oven and continue baking for 10 minutes.
11. Cool to room temperature, then refrigerate until chilled before serving.

Makes 8 servings.

Each serving contains:
- **152** *calories*
- **9** *grams protein*
- **13** *grams carbohydrate*
- **7** *grams fat*
- **276** *mg. sodium*
- **14** *mg. cholesterol*
- *negligible grams fiber*

ADA Exchange Value
- **1** *Lean Meat*
- **1** *Fruit*
- **$^1/_2$** *Fat*
- **41%** *of total calories are from fat.*

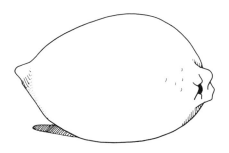

Lemon Yogurt Cake

These cakes are perfect for afternoon tea as well as a lovely dessert for a formal dinner party or casual entertaining. Store cake in refrigerator wrapped in foil or plastic wrap.

>   **4   tablespoons margarine**
> **$^1/_2$ cup fructose**
>   **6   egg whites**
>   **peel of 1 lemon, finely grated (see Tips)**
> **$^3/_4$ cup nonfat plain yogurt**
>   **2   cups self-raising presifted flour**
> **$^1/_2$ cup dried apricots, diced**

1. Preheat oven to 325 degrees.
2. Cream margarine and fructose until light and fluffy.
3. Add egg whites, 2 at a time, beating after each.
4. Fold in lemon peel, yogurt, flour and apricots.
5. Spoon mixture into loaf pan that has been sprayed with nonstick spray.
6. Bake 1 hour.

Makes 12 servings.

Each serving contains:
>   *159   calories*
>   *5   grams protein*
>   *11   grams carbohydrate*
>   *4   grams fat*
>   *325   mg. sodium*
>   *17   mg. cholesterol*
>   *1   gram fiber*

>   *ADA Exchange Value*
>   *1   Starch*
>   *1   Fat*
>   *23%   of calories are from fat.*

Almond Cake

Make Yogurt Cake omitting lemon peel and apricots. Add 1 oz. coarsely chopped almonds, 1 teaspoon vanilla and ½ teaspoon almond extract.

Makes 12 servings.

Each serving contains:
- *152 calories*
- *5 grams protein*
- *8 grams carbohydrate*
- *5 grams fat*
- *325 mg. sodium*
- *17 mg. cholesterol*
- *negligible grams fiber*

ADA Exchange Value
- *1 Starch*
- *1 Fat*
- *27% of calories are from fat.*

Chocolate Prune Cake

Sounds strange? But tastes great! Prunes add moisture and sweetness. A hint would be to chop prunes up small so your guests won't know the secret to this cake. If they knew beforehand, they might have a preconceived idea of prunes!

1 *cup whole pitted prunes*
4 *tablespoons margarine*
$2/3$ *cup fructose*
$1/8$ *cup molasses*
4 *egg whites*
$1/2$ *cup imported cocoa*
2 *cups self-rising flour*
$1/2$ *teaspoon ground cloves*
$1/2$ *cup water from cooking prunes*

1. Preheat oven to 350 degrees.
2. In a sauce pan, simmer prunes in 2 cups water for 10 minutes.
3. Drain water, reserving $1/2$ cup.
4. Coarsely chop prunes.
5. Cream margarine, fructose and molasses.
6. Add egg whites and beat well.
7. Sift in flour, cocoa and ground cloves.
8. Stir in prunes and prune liquid.
9. Pour in loaf pan sprayed with nonstick cooking spray. Bake 50 minutes.

Makes 10 servings.

Each serving contains:

		ADA Exchange Value
136	*calories*	1 *Starch*
5	*grams protein*	1 *Fat*
17	*grams carbohydrate*	34% *of total calories are*
5	*grams fat*	*from fat.*
307	*mg. sodium*	
21	*mg. cholesterol*	
1	*gram fiber*	

Section II
French

French Cuisine

French cuisine is known for its perfection. It pleases both the eye and the palate. Flavors are soft and delicate.

Traditionally, French food has been heavy in fats, using butter, heavy cream and lard unsparingly. However, with a few modifications, we can eliminate most of the fats and a lot of the time it takes in preparation.

When planning your French lunch, brunch or dinner parties, you can make it very formal using table settings in black, white and silver, with candles and small vases filled with a single rose. To make your meal very informal, use a country setting atmosphere with red and white tablecloths and napkins.

France is also known for wine and champagne. Always remember to cook with the wine you are serving. If you are not serving wine, but your recipe calls for it, select a dry vermouth.

THE PLEASURE OF YOUR COMPANY WITH FRENCH CUISINE

Formal Dinner Party

Table setting of white and black table linen.
Use black candles and small individual vases
with single red roses.
Use napkin rings.
Serve appetizers with cocktails in the living room.

MENU

Appetizers
Pate
Crudities

Cocktail
Kir Royal

Soup
French Onion

Salad
Caesar

Main Course
Coq au Vin
French Cut Green Beans

Dessert
Floating Island
Coffee

Serve coffee in the living room.

Informal French Luncheon

Table setting with red and white
checkered table cloth and/or napkins.
Put bread sticks in glasses on table.

Soup
Tomato and Carrot
Bread Sticks

Main Dish
Chicken Cakes
Molded Rice

Dessert
Pears a la Cream
Coffee

Pate

4 *green onions, including tops, chopped fine*
2 *tablespoons diet margarine*
1 1/2 *pounds chicken livers*
1/2 *teaspoon salt*
2 *teaspoons dry mustard*
1/2 *teaspoon ground nutmeg*
1/4 *teaspoon ground cloves*
8 *ounces neufchatel*
1/4 *cup cognac*

1. In a large skillet, melt margarine. Add green onions and saute until tender.
2. Add chicken livers, salt, mustard, nutmeg and cloves. Cover and cook on low for 10 to 15 minutes, until livers are cooked.
3. Place in food processor with steel blade or in a blender at high speed. While running, process in neufchatel, then cognac.
4. Pour mixture in a souffle dish or a pate tureen. Chill for at least 24 hours before serving.

Makes 12 servings.

Each serving contains:
147 *calories*
12 *grams protein*
2 *grams carbohydrate*
9 *grams fat*
189 *mg. sodium*
278 *mg. cholesterol*
negligible grams fiber

ADA Exchange Value
1 *Medium Fat Meat*
1 *Fat*
54% *of total calories are from fat.*

Tomato Carrot Soup

1   small sweet potato
1   tablespoon unsalted corn oil margarine
1   medium onion, chopped
3   15 oz. cans diced tomatoes in puree
1   glove garlic, minced
$1/2$ cup fresh chervil (1 tablespoon dried)
$1/4$ cup parsley, chopped
3   medium carrots, sliced
$1/2$ teaspoon fructose
$1/2$ teaspoon ground white pepper
4   cups Chicken Broth (page 124)
    fresh parsley to garnish

1. Bake sweet potato 45 minutes at 375 degrees. Peel and cut into cubes.
2. In a large Dutch oven, melt margarine over medium heat. Add onion and saute until soft.
3. Add tomatoes and garlic. Simmer for 15 minutes.
4. Add chervil, parsley, carrots, fructose and white pepper. Cover and cook on low until carrots are tender, 15 to 20 minutes.
5. Transfer the vegetables to a food processor or blender. Add sweet potato and blend until smooth (may have to be done in two batches).
6. Return to Dutch oven. Add Chicken Broth and heat on medium heat until warm.
7. Garnish with fresh parsley.

Makes 8 servings.

Each serving contains:

- **99** *calories*
- **3** *grams protein*
- **18** *grams carbohydrate*
- **2** *grams fat*
- **981** *mg. sodium*
- *negligible mg. cholesterol*
- **4** *grams fiber*

ADA Exchange Value

- **3** *Vegetable*
- **¹/₂** *Fat*
- **21%** *of total calories are from fat.*

French Onion Soup

This soup is a meal in itself and makes a perfect lunch or light dinner when served with a green salad and fruit.

1 1/2 **pounds yellow onions, peeled, cut in half and thinly sliced**
1/2 **teaspoon black pepper**
2 **tablespoons all-purpose flour**
9 **cups low-salt beef broth**
1 **tablespoon cognac (optional)**
6 **1/2 -inch slices toasted French bread**
6 **oz. grated low-fat cheese**

1. Cook onions and black pepper on low for 15 minutes in a large covered sauce pan that has been sprayed with a nonstick cooking spray, stirring occasionally.
2. Uncover, raise heat to medium and continue stirring until onions are light brown.
3. Sprinkle flour over onions and stir for about 3 minutes.
4. Add beef broth. Simmer, partially covered for 45 minutes. (This can be held at this point. When ready to serve, reheat to simmer.)
5. Add cognac. Stir in well.
6. Place french bread slices on a cookie sheet. Put 1 oz. of grated cheese on each. Put under broiler for 30 seconds.
7. Place the bread slices in 6 serving bowls. Ladle soup on top.

Makes 6 servings.

Each serving contains:

- *164   calories*
- *10   grams protein*
- *19   grams carbohydrate*
- *5   grams fat*
- *221   mg. sodium*
- *16   mg. cholesterol*
- *2   grams fiber*

ADA Exchange Value
- *1   Starch*
- *1   Medium Fat Meat*
- *29%   of total calories are from fat.*

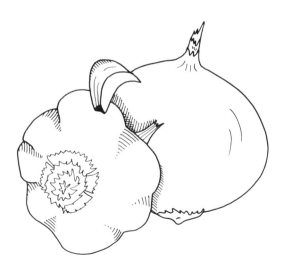

French Potato Salad

French potato salad is prepared while the potatoes are warm so they will absorb the dressing. You can serve it either warm or cold.

> **2 pounds small red potatoes, washed**
> **1/2 cup Vinaigrette Dressing (page 29)**
> **1 teaspoon Dijon mustard**
> **1 tablespoon parsley**

1. Boil potatoes until just tender when pierced with a knife.
2. Drain. As soon as you can handle them, cut into fourths or in slices.
3. Mix mustard into dressing.
4. Place potatoes in mixing bowl, pour dressing over and toss gently.
5. Sprinkle with fresh parsley before serving.

Makes 8 servings.

Each serving contains:
> **162 calories**
> **3 grams protein**
> **34 grams carbohydrate**
> **2 grams fat**
> **14 mg. sodium**
> **0 mg. cholesterol**
> **4 grams fiber**

> **ADA Exchange Value**
> **2 Starch**
> **10% of total calories are from fat**

Tomato Salad

3 *large tomatoes*
3 *scallions, washed, trimmed and chopped*
2 *tablespoons fresh parsley, chopped*
3 *tablespoons fresh lemon juice*
1 *teaspoon oregano*
$^1/_2$ *teaspoon ground black pepper*
$^1/_4$ *cup olive oil*

1. Cut tomatoes in eighths.
2. Mix all other ingredients and gently toss in tomatoes.

Makes 6 servings.

Each serving contains:
   96 *calories*
      negligible grams protein
    4 *grams carbohydrate*
    9 *grams fat*
    7 *mg. sodium*
    0 *mg. cholesterol*
    1 *gram fiber*

      ADA Exchange Value
    1 *Vegetable*
    2 *Fat*
 86% *of total calories are from fat*

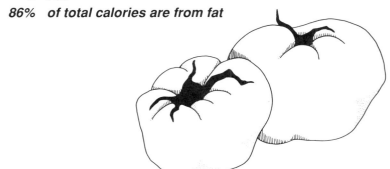

Tomato Cucumber Salad

1   **cucumber, peeled and sliced**
1   **large tomato, sliced**
4   **romaine leaves, washed and patted dry**
$^1/_2$ **cup Basil Dressing (page 31)**

1. Marinate cucumber and tomato in Basil Dressing for 2 hours.
2. On 4 salad plates, place 1 romaine leaf each and $^1/_4$ of marinated cucumbers and tomatoes.

Makes 4 servings.

Each serving contains:
> 85   *calories*
> 1   *gram protein*
> 6   *grams carbohydrate*
> 7   *grams fat*
> 29   *mg. sodium*
> 0   *mg. cholesterol*
> 2   *grams fiber*
>
> *ADA Exchange Value*
> 1   *Vegetable*
> 1   *Fat*
> 74%   *of total calories are from fat.*

Bib Lettuce With Radishes

2   *heads bib lettuce*
1   *bunch of radishes, thinly sliced*
1/2   *cup Vinaigrette Dressing (page 29)*

1. Wash bib lettuce. Drain and tear into bite-size pieces. Spin or pat dry.
2. Toss lettuce, radishes and dressing together and place on four salad plates.

Makes 4 servings.

Each serving contains:

    42   *calories*
          negligible grams protein
     3   *grams carbohydrate*
     4   *grams fat*
    16   *mg. sodium*
     0   *mg. cholesterol*
     1   *gram fiber*

          ADA Exchange Value
     1   *Vegetable*
     1   *Fat*
   75%   *of total calories are from fat.*

Spinach Salad With Strawberries

       2   *bunches fresh spinach*
     1/2 cup Poppy Seed Dressing (page 79)
      12   *strawberries, cut in half*

1. Wash spinach carefully as each leaf can hold dirt. Break the stems off the leaves. Spin or pat dry.
2. Toss spinach with dressing.
3. Place on four serving plates and garnish each with 6 strawberry halves.

Makes 4 servings.

Each serving contains:
     153 calories
       3 grams protein
       5 grams carbohydrate
      14 grams fat
      65 mg. sodium
       0 mg. cholesterol
       3 grams fiber

           ADA Exchange Value
       1 Vegetable
       3 Fat
     85% of total calories are from fat.

Poppy Seed Dressing
for Spinach Salad with Strawberries

1   *egg white*
1   *packet Equal,*™ *or* ¹/₂ *tablespoon fructose*
1 ¹/₂   *teaspoons dijon style mustard*
¹/₄   *cup raspberry vinegar (or apple cider vinegar)*
¹/₄   *cup water*
¹/₂   *cup corn oil*
1   *tablespoon poppy seeds*

1. Combine egg white, Equal™, mustard, vinegar and water in blender.
2. While blender is running, slowly drizzle in corn oil. Blend until well mixed.
3. Pour into storage container and add 1 tablespoon poppy seeds.
4. Makes 1 cup.

Makes 8 servings. 1 serving = 2 tablespoons

Each serving contains:
132   *calories*
1   *gram protein*
1   *gram carbohydrate*
14   *grams fat*
20   *mg. sodium*
0   *mg. cholesterol*
negligible grams fiber

ADA Exchange Value
3   *Fat*
96%   *of total calories are from fat.*

Pepper and Cucumber Salad

Dressing:
- 1 cup fresh orange juice
- ¹/₄ cup fresh lemon juice
- 1 tablespoon olive oil
- 1 clove garlic, crushed
- ¹/₂ teaspoon white pepper
- ¹/₄ cup fresh basil, washed, dried and cut in julienne strips

Salad:
- 2 whole peppers, red, green and/or yellow, roasted, skinned and cut in julienne strips (see Tips)
- 1 cucumber, peeled, cut in half, seeded, sliced thin
- 2 tomatoes, skinned, seeded, cut in julienne strips
- 1 bunch red leaf lettuce, washed and dried (see Tips)

1. Marinate pepper, cucumbers and tomatoes in dressing in refrigerator 2 to 6 hours.
2. Drain vegetables, reserving dressing.
3. Toss dressing in lettuce and divide among 6 salad plates.
4. Divide marinated vegetables in 6 and place on top of lettuce.

Makes 6 servings.

Each serving contains:
- 66 calories
- 2 grams protein
- 10 grams carbohydrate
- 3 grams fat
- 11 mg. sodium
- 0 mg. cholesterol
- 2 grams fiber
- *ADA Exchange Value*
- 2 Vegetable
- ¹/₂ Fat
- 37% of total calories are from fat.

THE GUILTLESS GOURMET GOES ETHNIC

Salad Nicoise

This is a perfect main course summer salad. You can have all the ingredients ready in advance so all you have to do is arrange it any way you wish.

  1 *head Boston lettuce, separated, washed and dried*
  3 *cups green beans, cooked and chilled*
  3 *tomatoes, quartered*
  3 *cups chilled French Potato Salad (page 74)*
  2 *6 ¹/₂ oz. water packed solid tuna, drained*
  3 *hard boiled eggs, quartered*
  3 *teaspoons capers*
  2 *tablespoons chopped fresh parsley*
 12 *tablespoons Vinaigrette Dressing (page 29)*

1. Either arrange salad on six salad plates or in 1 large salad bowl.
2. Pour dressing over the top of the salad.

Makes 6 servings.

Each serving contains:
- 285 *calories*
- 23 *grams protein*
- 32 *grams carbohydrate*
- 8 *grams fat*
- 261 *mg. sodium*
- 160 *mg. cholesterol*
- 5 *grams fiber*

   ADA Exchange Value
- 2 *Starch*
- 2 *Lean Meat*
- 25% *of total calories are from fat.*

Orange and Lemon Salad

3 tablespoons olive oil
$^1/_4$ cup fresh lemon juice
1 teaspoon fructose
1 teaspoon bitters
$^1/_8$ teaspoon ground black pepper
    large bunch water cress, washed, dried
    and tough stems removed
3 large oranges, peeled and sliced $^1/_4$ inch
1 lemon, peeled and sliced $^1/_8$ inch
3 tablespoons golden raisins
$^1/_4$ cup walnuts, chopped

1. Mix olive oil, lemon juice, fructose, bitters and black pepper together.
2. Divide water cress among 6 plates. Arrange orange and lemon slices on each.
3. Pour dressing over each. Sprinkle each with raisins and walnuts.

Makes 6 servings.

Each serving contains:
   155 *calories*
     3 *grams protein*
   17 *grams carbohydrate*
   10 *grams fat*
     7 *mg. sodium*
     0 *mg. cholesterol*
     4 *grams fiber*

     ADA Exchange Value
     1 *Fruit*
     2 *Fat*
 57% *of total calories are from fat.*

Molded Brown Rice

2 *cups short grain brown rice, uncooked*
1 *red bell pepper, diced*
5 *cups Chicken Broth (page 124)*
fresh parsley to garnish

1. Put all ingredients in rice cooker and cook until done or in a sauce pan bring liquid to boil. Add rice and bell pepper. Cover and simmer until done (about 45 minutes).
2. Place cooked rice in a 5 cup mold that has been sprayed with a vegetable spray and press down firmly. (This can be made ahead and reheated.)
3. Place mold in oven at 350 degrees for 10 minutes. Unmold on serving platter and garnish with fresh parsley.

Makes 8 servings.

Each serving contains:
    79 *calories*
     2 *grams protein*
   16 *grams carbohydrate*
     1 *gram fat*
 566 *mg. sodium*
       negligible mg. cholesterol
     1 *gram fiber*

       ADA Exchange Value
     1 *Starch*
       negligible fat calories.

Peasant Risotto

This is a great one-dish dinner. It's also a great way to use leftovers.

> 2   *tablespoons margarine*
> 1   *medium onion, chopped*
> 1   *green or red bell pepper*
> 1/2 *pound mushrooms, sliced*
> 2   *cups rice**
> 1   *pound cooked chicken breast, cubed*
> 4   *cups Chicken Broth (page 124)*

1. In a small Dutch oven, melt margarine on medium high heat.
2. Add onion and bell pepper. Cook until soft.
3. Add mushrooms. Cover 3 minutes. Uncover and continue cooking until liquid is absorbed.
4. Add rice and saute until all rice is coated.
5. Add Chicken Broth. Bring to boil. Reduce heat to low. Cover and cook until all liquid is absorbed.

*If using brown rice, it may need more liquid. Check instructions on the rice package.

Makes 6 servings.

Each serving contains:

> 295   *calories*
> 25   *grams protein*
> 19   *grams carbohydrate*
> 13   *grams fat*
> 1006   *mg. sodium*
> 65   *mg. cholesterol*
> 2   *grams fiber*

> *ADA Exchange Value*
> 3   *Lean Meat*
> 1   *Starch*
> 1   *Fat*
> 40%   *of total calories are from fat.*

French Brussels Sprouts

1 pound fresh brussels sprouts, washed and trimmed (or 2 packages frozen and thawed)
1/2 cup Chicken Broth (page 124)
1 tablespoon dry Butter Buds™

1. Steam brussels sprouts until crisp tender (3 to 5 minutes).
2. In a nonstick skillet, reduce 1/4 cup Chicken Broth down to 1 tablespoon.
3. Mix dry Butter Buds™ with remaining 1/4 cup Chicken Broth. Add to the pan and reduce by 1/2.
4. Cut brussels sprouts in half. Add to pan and saute until all are well coated and hot.

Makes 4 servings.

Each serving contains:
- *41 calories*
- *3 grams protein*
- *8 grams carbohydrate*
- *negligible grams fat*
- *237 mg. sodium*
- *negligible mg. cholesterol*
- *1 gram fiber*

ADA Exchange Value
1 1/2 Vegetable
negligible fat calories.

Crepes Coquilles St. Jacques

Court Bouillon

   1   small onion, sliced
   1   stalk celery, cut up
   1   bay leaf
   3   slices lemon
   1   cup water
  $^1/_2$ cup dry white wine
   1   pound sea scallops, washed and drained

Sauce

  $^1/_4$ cup chopped onion
  $^1/_2$ pound mushrooms, sliced
  $^1/_4$ cup flour
  $^1/_4$ teaspoon white pepper
   1   cup 1% milk
   6   oz. gruyere cheese
  $^1/_2$ cup Court Bouillon
   2   tablespoons dry white wine
   1   tablespoon chopped parsley
       parsley to garnish
  12   Crepes (page 89)

Court Bouillon

1. In a medium sauce pan, combine all ingredients except wine and bring to boil. Simmer for 10 minutes.
2. Add wine and sea scallops. Cover and simmer for 6 minutes or until tender. Drain, reserve liquid.

Sauce

1. Put 2 tablespoons Court Bouillon in skillet. Bring to boil. Add onions. Saute 1 minute stirring constantly. Add mushrooms. Reduce heat. Cover until mushrooms are soft. Remove cover. Saute until all liquid is absorbed.
2. Mix flour, pepper and milk. Pour into onions and mushrooms. Stir until thick.

3. Add gruyere cheese. Stir until melted. Turn off heat. Add wine, ¹/₂ cup Court Bouillon, parsley and scallops. Mix well.
4. Divide scallops into 12 portions. Wrap them in Crepes with a small amount of sauce. Place them on a serving platter or on 6 plates — 2 per serving.
5. Spoon sauce across the middle of Crepes. Garnish with parsley.

Makes 6 servings.

Each serving contains:
- 488 *calories*
- 43 *grams protein*
- 46 *grams carbohydrate*
- 13 *grams fat*
- 676 *mg. sodium*
- 173 *mg. cholesterol*
- 2 *grams fiber*

   ADA Exchange Value
- 5 *Lean Meat*
- 2 *Starch*
- 2 *Vegetable*
- 23% *of total calories are from fat.*

Salmon Omelet Souffle

This is a quick and tasty dish that is also good served cold.

> 1   *7 ³/₄ ounce can of salmon*
> 2   *eggs*
> 2   *egg whites*
> 2   *tablespoons tomato paste*
> ¹/₄   *cup green onion, chopped*
> ¹/₈   *teaspoon dill weed*

1. Preheat oven to 350 degrees.
2. Beat eggs until frothy. Fold in the rest of ingredients.
3. Pour in 9-inch baking dish that has been sprayed with nonstick spray.
4. Bake for 20 minutes or until done.

Makes 3 servings.

Each serving contains:
> *153   calories*
> *18   grams protein*
> *3   grams carbohydrate*
> *7   grams fat*
> *411   mg. sodium*
> *208   mg. cholesterol*
> *1   gram fiber*
>
> *ADA Exchange Value*
> *2   Lean Meat*
> *¹/₂   Vegetable*
> *¹/₂   Fat*
> *44%   of total calories are from fat.*

Crepes

Almost anything can go into a crepe and become an attractive, nourishing main course, sort of a French burrito!

This is a basic recipe that will make 12 6-inch crepes. You can make them ahead and freeze them with sheets of wax paper between each one.

> **2 cups cold nonfat milk**
> **2 eggs + 4 egg whites**
> **2 cups unbleached white flour**

1. Put ingredients in a blender and blend at top speed for 1 minute, scraping down sides of blender.
2. Cover and refrigerate for at least 2 hours.
3. Heat a 6 1/2 inch to 7 inch skillet. Spray with a nonstick coating.
4. Pour 1/4 cup batter into pan. Pick up pan and roll around covering bottom of pan. Return pan to heat for about 60 to 80 seconds. Then jerk and toss pan sharply back and forth to loosen the crepe. Then turn or flip crepe over and cook 30 seconds. (If crepe seems to thick, add water, 1 tablespoon at a time.)

Makes 12 crepes. 1 serving = 1 crepe

Each serving contains:
- 103 *calories*
- 6 *grams protein*
- 17 *grams carbohydrate*
- 1 *gram fat*
- 50 *mg. sodium*
- 46 *mg. cholesterol*
- *negligible grams fiber*

ADA Exchange Value
- 1 *Starch*
- 1/2 *Lean Meat*
- 10% *of total calories are from fat.*

THE GUILTLESS GOURMET GOES ETHNIC

Quiche

This can be a very versatile dish. You can use any leftover vegetables. Be creative and have fun!

$^1/_4$ **cup chicken broth**
$^1/_2$ **teaspoon garlic, minced**
2 **medium zucchini, shredded and well drained**
2 **tablespoons Parmesan cheese, grated**
$^1/_2$ **pound broccoli, chopped and steamed**
1 $^1/_4$ **cup nonfat milk + 3 tablespoons nonfat dry milk powder**
3 **oz. low-fat cheese, shredded**
2 **eggs, separated**
1 **egg white**
2 **tablespoons tomato paste**
1 **tablespoon dried basil leaves, crushed dash red pepper**

1. Preheat oven to 350 degrees.
2. Reduce chicken broth in a nonstick skillet to 1 tablespoon. Add minced garlic and saute 1 minute. Add shredded zucchini and cook about 3 minutes. Add 1 tablespoon Parmesan cheese and cook 1 more minute.
3. Spray the bottom of an 8 inch quiche pan with a nonstick spray. Spread vegetable mixture thinly on the bottom of the pan to form a crust.
4. Arrange broccoli on top, sprinkle with shredded lowfat cheese.
5. Mix nonfat milk, nonfat milk powder and egg yolks.
6. Add tomato paste, basil leaves and red pepper.
7. Beat egg whites until stiff and fold into milk mixture.
8. Pour mixture into quiche pan and sprinkle with 1 tablespoon of parmesan cheese.
9. Bake for 30 minutes or until set in center.

Makes 4 servings.

Each serving contains:

- *191 calories*
- *17 grams protein*
- *14 grams carbohydrate*
- *8 grams fat*
- *350 mg. sodium*
- *155 mg. cholesterol*
- *4 grams fiber*

ADA Exchange Value

- *1 Medium Fat Meat*
- *1 Vegetable*
- *1/2 Nonfat Milk*
- *1 Fat*
- *38% of total calories are from fat.*

Souffle

This is an out-of-the-ordinary souffle because you don't have to serve it immediately in fear of it falling. This is unmolded so it makes a nice appearance. It can be kept warm or reheated. It makes a nice first course for 8 or main course for 4.

2 1/2 **tablespoons low calorie margarine**
3 **tablespoons flour**
3/4 **cup hot nonfat milk**
1/4 **teaspoon white pepper**
2 **egg yolks**
6 **egg whites**
1/4 **teaspoon cream of tartar**
1 **oz. grated Parmesan cheese**
3 **oz. lowfat cheddar cheese**
10 **oz. frozen chopped spinach, thawed and water squeezed out**
8 **oz. fresh mushrooms, sliced and cooked (see Tips)**

1. Preheat oven to 350 degrees.
2. Have ready a 2-quart straight-sided baking dish that has been sprayed with a nonstick cooking spray and the 1 oz. Parmesan cheese rolled around covering bottom and sides.
3. Also have ready a larger baking dish to hold water and set the dish that holds the souffle. Water should come up 1/2 of the souffle dish.
4. Melt margarine in sauce pan. Add flour. Stir slowly over low heat for 2 minutes, not letting it brown.
5. Slowly stir in hot milk. Bring to boil, stirring vigorously with a wire whip. Mixture will be very thick.
6. Remove from heat. Add white pepper.
7. Add egg yolks to mixture and beat in well.
8. Place egg whites in a clean bowl and whip at moderate speed until they begin to froth.
9. Add cream of tartar to egg whites and beat at high speed until they form stiff peaks.

10. Stir ¹/₄ of egg whites into hot mixture to lighten it.
11. Stir in the cheddar cheese, mushrooms and spinach.
12. Fold in the rest of the egg whites quickly with a rubber spatula taking about 30 seconds.
13. Put the mixture in the prepared souffle dish. Place that dish in the dish with hot water and bake slowly for 1 ¹/₄ hours. Souffle will be brown on top with slight shrinkage from the dish.
14. Unmold by turning on to a serving platter.
15. May be garnished with fresh parsley and diced tomatoes.

Makes 4 servings.

Each serving contains:
- 280 *calories*
- 18 *grams protein*
- 13 *grams carbohydrate*
- 18 *grams fat*
- 347 *mg. sodium*
- 161 *mg. cholesterol*
- 3 *grams fiber*

ADA Exchange Value
- 1 *Starch*
- 2 *Medium Fat Meat*
- 1 *Fat*
- 58% *of total calories are from fat.*

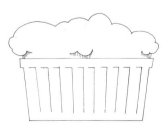

Baked Chicken

2 teaspoons rosemary
1/2 teaspoon Italian seasoning
3 cloves of garlic, crushed
6 chicken breasts with bone and skin removed
1/2 cup dry white wine
1 cup Chicken Broth (page 124)
fresh parsley for garnish

1. Preheat oven to 400 degrees.
2. Mix rosemary, Italian seasoning and garlic together well in a mortar and pastel or mini food chopper.
3. Rub seasonings on chicken breast.
4. Place in a baking dish. Bake for 15 minutes.
5. Pour wine and Chicken Broth over chicken. Cover and bake 20 to 30 minutes longer (until done).
6. Place chicken on serving platter and garnish with fresh parsley.

Makes 6 servings.

Each serving contains:
188 calories
33 grams protein
1 gram carbohydrate
5 grams fat
301 mg. sodium
88 mg. cholesterol
negligible grams fiber

ADA Exchange Value
4 Lean Meat
22% of total calories are from fat.

Coq Au Vin

6 chicken breasts with bone and skin removed
12 small pearl onions, peeled
12 small new potatoes
6 medium carrots, cleaned and sliced in
   $1/2$ inch rounds
4 stalks celery, cleaned and sliced in
   $1/2$ inch diagonals
6 tablespoons flour
1 teaspoon garlic powder
1 teaspoon rosemary
1 teaspoon black pepper, ground
$1 1/2$ cups Chicken Broth (page 124)
$1/4$ cup tomato paste
2 shallots
1 pound large mushrooms, cleaned and quartered
2 cups good red wine
1 large cooking bag

1. Shake in large cooking bag the chicken, onions, potatoes, carrots, celery, 4 tablespoons flour, garlic, rosemary, thyme and pepper.
2. Mix tomato paste with Chicken Broth and pour over chicken and vegetables.
3. Seal cooking bag and make 2 slits in bag.
4. Bake 2 $1/2$ hours at 350 degrees.
5. Remove chicken and vegetables to baking dish and drain broth in a bowl and degrease.
6. Put defatted broth in large pan and heat.
7. Add 2 chopped shallots and mushrooms and cook until done.
8. Mix 2 tablespoons flour in $1/4$ cup water and stir into mixture to thicken.
9. Add wine and stir in well.
10. Pour over chicken and vegetables and bake at 350 degrees for $1/2$ hour.

Makes 6 servings.

Each serving contains:
- *416 calories*
- *39 grams protein*
- *41 grams carbohydrate*
- *5 grams fat*
- *480 mg. sodium*
- *88 mg. cholesterol*
- *6 grams fiber*

ADA Exchange Value
- *2 Starch*
- *2 Vegetable*
- *4 Lean Meat*
- *11% of total calories are from fat.*

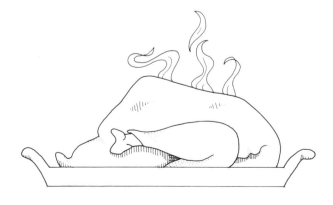

Chicken With Lemon and Capers

1 tablespoon olive oil
1 medium onion, sliced
3 cloves garlic, chopped
6 4 oz. chicken breasts, boned and skinned
2 cups dry white wine
2 lemons, sliced very thin with skins
2 tablespoons small capers
1/4 cup fresh chopped parsley
3 cups cooked brown rice

1. In a large skillet or Dutch oven, heat olive oil. Add onion and garlic. Saute until tender.
2. Add chicken breasts and brown on both sides.
3. Add wine. Bring to a quick boil. Reduce heat to simmer.
4. Add lemons and capers. Cover and simmer until chicken is done (about 8 to 10 minutes). Add parsley.
5. Serve over brown rice.

Makes 6 servings.

Each serving contains:
384 calories
36 grams protein
30 grams carbohydrate
7 grams fat
694 mg. sodium
88 mg. cholesterol
1 gram fiber

ADA Exchange Value
2 Starch
4 Lean Meat
16% of total calories are from fat.

Mustard Chicken

6 boneless, skinless chicken breasts
$^1/_2$ cup Dijon mustard
$^1/_4$ cup white wine vinegar
1 clove garlic, crushed
$^1/_4$ teaspoon crushed thyme

Sauce

1 cup Chicken Broth (page 124)
1 tablespoon arrowroot
$^1/_2$ cup lowfat sour cream
$^1/_4$ cup dijon mustard

1. Combine mustard, wine vinegar, garlic and thyme. Pour over chicken to marinate 2 to 6 hours.
2. Grill or broil until done. Place on serving platter and keep warm.
3. Make sauce by mixing arrowroot into Chicken Broth.
4. Heat until thickened.
5. Stir in sour cream and mustard.
6. Spoon sauce over chicken breast.

Makes 6 servings.

Each serving contains:
217 calories
34 grams protein
4 grams carbohydrate
6 grams fat
690 mgs. sodium
88 mgs. cholesterol
1 gram fiber

ADA Exchange Value
4 Lean Meat
$^1/_2$ Starch
25% of total calories are from fat.

Chicken Cakes With Tomato and Sweet Pepper Sauce

Chicken Cakes

- 1 1/2 **pounds boned and skinned chicken breasts**
- 1 **cup chopped red pepper**
- 1/2 **cup chopped celery**
- 6 **green onions, chopped**
- 2 **cups fine dried bread crumbs**
- 2 **egg whites**
- 1/2 **cup nonfat milk**
- 2 **tablespoons Dijon-style mustard**
- 1/4 **cup chopped fresh parsley**
- 2 **tablespoons chopped fresh tarragon or 2 teaspoons dried**
- 1/2 **teaspoon ground black pepper**

Tomato and Sweet Pepper Sauce

- 2 **shallots, chopped**
- 1 **red bell pepper, seeded and chopped**
- 3 **14 1/2 oz. cans diced tomatoes in juice**
- 1/4 **cup dry white vermouth**
- 1/2 **cup fresh chopped parsley**
- 1 **tablespoon fresh tarragon or 1 teaspoon dried**
- 1/2 **teaspoon cayenne pepper**

Chicken Cakes
1. Put chicken breasts in food processor. With quick on-off, coarsely chop.
2. In a skillet sprayed with nonstick spray, saute celery, green onion and red pepper until tender.
3. In mixing bowl, add chicken. Cook vegetables, bread crumbs, egg whites, mustard, parsley, milk, tarragon and pepper. Mix together well and chill for at least 2 hours.
4. Form into 16 cakes. Place on cookie sheet sprayed with a nonstick spray. Bake in 400 degree oven for 15 minutes.

5. Place ¹/₂ the tomato and sweet pepper sauce in cook-and-serve baking dish. Place the chicken cakes on sauce and bake in a 350 degree oven covered for ¹/₂ hour.
6. Either serve from baking dish at the table or place on individual plates, 2 per serving. Pass the remaining sauce at the table.

Tomato Sweet Pepper Sauce
1. Saute shallots and sweet pepper until tender in a skillet sprayed with a nonstick spray.
2. Add tomatoes and simmer uncovered 8 to 10 minutes, stirring occasionally.
3. Stir in wine and continue simmering until sauce thickens (about 15 minutes).
4. Add tarragon, parsley and cayenne pepper.

Makes 8 servings.

Each serving contains:
- *334 calories*
- *34 grams protein*
- *36 grams carbohydrate*
- *5 grams fat*
- *632 mg. sodium*
- *69 mgs cholesterol*
- *4 grams fiber*

ADA Exchange Value
- *4 Lean Meat*
- *2 Starch*
- *1 Vegetable*
- *15% of total calories are from fat.*

Sole

This is a delicate dish that is perfect served with molded rice.

6 *filets of sole (2 1/2 pounds)*
2 *tablespoons lemon juice*
1 *clove garlic, crushed*
1/2 *teaspoon dried tarragon leaves*
1/2 *teaspoon dried basil leaves*
1 *cup dry white wine*

Sauce

1 *cup + 3 tablespoons liquid from cooking fish*
1 *shallot, chopped*
1 *tablespoon chopped parsley*
1 *tablespoon flour*
3 *tablespoons tomato paste*
1/8 *teaspoon cayenne*
2/3 *cup nonfat milk*
1/4 *cup dry white wine*
1/2 *pound shrimp, cooked and cleaned*

1. Brush both sides of sole with lemon juice. Cut lengthwise. Roll up with dark side to the inside. Arrange standing up in a single layer in a large skillet.
2. Mix garlic, tarragon and basil in the wine. Pour over fish. Bring to boil. Reduce to simmer and cover 10 to 12 minutes.
3. Remove filets from skillet with a slotted spoon to a warm serving platter. Cover and keep warm.
4. Strain the cooking liquid and measure 1 cup + 3 tablespoons (if there is not enough, add water to make up the difference).

Sauce
1. Place 3 tablespoons cooking liquid from fish in the skillet. Bring to a boil. Add shallot and parsley. Reduce heat and saute 1 minute.
2. Mix flour, tomato paste, cayenne and milk into the remaining cooking liquid. Bring to boil, cooking until thick and smooth.

3. Add wine and shrimp and heat.
4. Pour sauce over filets and serve.

Makes 6 servings.

Each serving contains:
- 239 *calories*
- 37 *grams protein*
- 10 *grams carbohydrate*
- 2 *grams fat*
- 188 *mg. sodium*
- 131 *mg. cholesterol*
- 1 *gram fiber*

ADA Exchange Value
- 4 *Lean Meat*
- 2 *Vegetable*
- 7% *of total calories are from fat.*

Pepper Steak

This sirloin steak can be barbequed for a casual Sunday afternoon or can be broiled and sliced for a formal Saturday dinner.

2 pounds boneless sirloin steak
2 teaspoons coarsely ground black pepper
parsley to garnish

1. Sprinkle both sides of steak with pepper. Using a rolling pin, press in well.
2. Barbeque or broil until the desired doneness.
3. Let stand 10 minutes. Slice in thin slices.

Makes 6 servings.

Each serving contains:
- **327 calories**
- **31 grams protein**
- **0 grams carbohydrate**
- **21 grams fat**
- **70 mg. sodium**
- **103 mg. cholesterol**
- **0 grams fiber**

ADA Exchange Value
4 Medium Fat Meat
58% of total calories are from fat.

Beef Stroganoff

This is quick and easy to prepare and always a favorite when company comes to dinner. Serve with rice or noodles.

- 1 *pound beef sirloin steak, trim and cut in strips*
- 1/2 *medium onion, cut in thin strips*
- 1 *cup beef broth, low salt*
- 1 *pound sliced mushrooms*
- 3 *teaspoons arrowroot*
- 1/4 *teaspoon ground black pepper*
- 1/4 *cup dry white vermouth*
- 1 *cup lowfat sour cream*

1. In a skillet sprayed with nonstick spray, brown meat on all sides on high heat. Remove from skillet. Set aside.
2. Heat 1/4 cup of beef broth in skillet. Add onions. Cook until soft on medium heat. Add mushrooms. Cover and simmer 5 minutes. Remove cover and continue cooking until all liquid is absorbed, stirring constantly.
3. Add vermouth. Bring quickly to boil, then reduce heat to simmer
4. Mix arrowroot in beef broth. Add to skillet. Stir until thickened.
5. Add beef and pepper.
6. Gently stir in sour cream.

Each serving contains: Makes 6 servings.
- 264 *calories*
- 25 *grams protein*
- 6 *grams carbohydrate*
- 15 *grams fat*
- 319 *mg. sodium*
- 67 *mg. cholesterol*
- 0.7 *gram fiber*

ADA Exchange Value
- 3 *Lean Meat*
- 1 *Vegetable*
- 1 *Fat*
- 48% *of total calories are from fat.*

Chicken Stroganoff

Use 1 pound chicken breasts sliced in strips and chicken broth instead of beef broth.

Makes 6 servings.

Each serving contains:
- 264 *calories*
- 25 *grams protein*
- 6 *grams carbohydrate*
- 15 *grams fat*
- 319 *mg. sodium*
- 67 *mg. cholesterol*
- 1 *gram fiber*

  ADA Exchange Value
- 3 *Lean Meat*
- 1 *Vegetable*
- 1 *Fat*
- 50% *of total calories are from fat.*

Beef Provencal

This great one dish meal is often referred to as farmers stew in France.

3 **pounds boneless chuck, trimmed of all fat and cut in 1 inch cubes**
1/2 **cup all purpose flour**
1/2 **teaspoon ground black pepper**
1 **leek, washed, trimmed of root and top green (see Tips), cut in rings**
8 **small white onions, peeled and cut in half**
1 **clove garlic, crushed**
2 **bay leaves**
1 **can (1 pound 12 oz.) tomatoes, undrained**
16 **small new potatoes, scrubbed, pare a strip of peel around each potato**
4 **zucchini (1 1/2 pounds) cut in 1 inch slices**
  chopped parsley
  large cooking bag
1/4 **cup all purpose flour mixed in 1/2 cup water**

Marinade
1 **teaspoon dried orange rind**
1 1/2 **cups dry red wine**
1 1/2 **tablespoon dried thyme leave flakes**

1. Mix marinade in large bowl. Place beef cubes in the bowl and toss to coat well. Marinate in refrigerator 2 to 3 hours or overnight.
2. Drain marinade from meat. Reserve marinade.
3. Place 1/2 cup of flour and pepper in cooking bag. Shake beef cubes in bag until all are covered.
4. Place leeks, onion and potatoes in cooking bag with meat.
5. Mix garlic, marinade and tomatoes together. Add bay leaves and pour over meat and vegetables.

6. Seal the bag closed and make 6 $\frac{1}{2}$ inch slits on top for steam to escape. Place in roasting pan and bake in a 300 degree oven for 4 hours.
7. Mix well $\frac{1}{4}$ cup flour with $\frac{1}{2}$ cup water. Set aside.
8. Drain liquid from bag in a sauce pan. Place meat mixture in a casserole pan that can also be served from.
9. Stir zucchini into meat mixture.
10. Heat liquid to boil. Add flour mixture. Stir to thicken.
11. Pour over stew and mix in.
12. Bake for 30 minutes covered. Uncover and bake another 15 minutes.
13. Sprinkle with chopped parsley.

Makes 10 servings.

Each serving contains:
- **456 calories**
- **36 grams protein**
- **29 grams carbohydrate**
- **17 grams fat**
- **221 mg. sodium**
- **108 mg. cholesterol**
- **4 grams fiber**

ADA Exchange Value
- **1 Starch**
- **2 Vegetable**
- **4 Medium Fat Meat**
- **33% of total calories are from fat.**

Chocolate Souffle

   1/4 **cup fructose**
   3 **tablespoons cornstarch**
   3 **tablespoons imported cocoa powder,**
      unsweetened
   1 **teaspoon instant coffee**
   1/4 **teaspoon cinnamon**
1 1/2 **cups 1% milk**
   1 **teaspoon vanilla**
   2 **egg whites**

1. Combine fructose, cornstarch, cocoa powder, instant coffee and cinnamon in a 2-quart sauce pan.
2. Add milk and cook over medium heat, stirring constantly until mixture comes to a boil and thickens.
3. Add vanilla.
4. Pour into a 1-quart bowl and cover surface of pudding with waxed paper to prevent "skin" formation.
5. Chill for 1 hour.
6. Beat egg whites until stiff.
7. Fold into chocolate mixture until fully incorporated.
8. Spoon into individual 4 ounce dessert dishes.

Makes 4 servings.

Each serving contains:
   125 **calories**
     6 **grams protein**
    19 **grams carbohydrate**
     2 **grams fat**
    87 **mg. sodium**
     6 **mg. cholesterol**
       negligible grams fiber

   ADA Exchange Value
   1/2 **1% Milk**
   1 **Starch**
 11% **of total calories are from fat.**

Cake Roll

This is a basic cake roll that you can roll up with a variety of fillings including low calorie jelly and preserves for the traditional jelly roll.

$3/4$ **cup unbleached pastry flour, sifted**
$3/4$ **teaspoon baking powder**
2 **whole eggs**
3 **egg whites**
2 **tablespoons fructose**
$1/4$ **teaspoon vanilla**

1. Preheat oven to 400 degrees.
2. Line a 11x16x$1/2$-inch jelly roll pan with waxed paper and spray with a nonstick spray.
3. Sift together flour and baking powder.
4. Whip whole eggs until fluffy. Gradually add fructose and vanilla and beat until very light and thick.
5. Fold flour mixture into eggs.
6. Spread evenly on jelly roll pan and bake 8 to 9 minutes or until cake springs back when pressed lightly in the center.
7. Let cake cool 2 to 3 minutes, then turn out onto a tea towel that has been lightly floured.
8. Remove wax paper (if cake is dry and crisp around edges, trim them).
9. Roll the cake in the tea towel and let cool.
10. When you are ready to fill the cake, unroll, but do not flatten edges. Spread with your filling and re-roll using the towel to help you.
11. Chill at least 2 hours before slicing.

Makes 12 servings.

Each serving contains:
- *50 calories*
- *3 grams protein*
- *7 grams carbohydrate*
- *1 gram fat*
- *51 mg. sodium*
- *16 mg. cholesterol*
- *negligible grams fiber*

ADA Exchange Value
- *1/2 Starch*
- *18% of total calories are from fat.*

Chocolate Roll

Use $^1/_2$ cup unbleached pastry flour with $^1/_4$ cup cocoa. Increase fructose to $^1/_2$ cup and vanilla to 1 teaspoon.

Makes 12 servings.

Each serving contains:
- 65   *calories*
- 3   *grams protein*
- 10   *grams carbohydrate*
- 1   *gram fat*
- 35   *mg. sodium*
- 47   *mg. cholesterol*
-     *negligible grams fiber*

    ADA Exchange Value
- $^3/_4$ *Starch*
- 17%   *of total calories are from fat.*

Black Forest Roll

1 *envelope gelatin*
1/4 *cup boiling water*
1 *cup evaporated skim milk, very cold*
1 *tablespoon imported cocoa powder*
1 *teaspoon instant coffee*
1/2 *teaspoon vanilla*
1 *tablespoon fructose or 2 packets Equal*™
20 *black cherries, pitted*
1 *Chocolate Cake Roll (page 111)*

1. Add boiling water to gelatin. Stir until dissolved. Set aside.
2. Whip chilled milk in a cold bowl with cold beaters until double in volume.
3. Add cocoa, instant coffee, vanilla and fructose or Equal™, while whipping.
4. Slowly pour in gelatin. Whip until slightly thick.
5. Put in refrigerator 15 minutes. Take out and stir (you don't want a lot of air in it).
6. Spread on Chocolate Cake Roll.
7. At the beginning of the roll, put a row of cherries.
8. Roll up the roll and refrigerate at least 2 hours before slicing.

Makes 12 servings.

Each serving contains:
102 *calories*
5 *grams protein*
15 *grams carbohydrate*
2 *grams fat*
53 *mg. sodium*
47 *mg. cholesterol*
negligible grams fiber

ADA Exchange Value
1 *Starch*
1/2 *Lean Meat*
13% *of total calories are from fat.*

Strawberry Crepes

     1   *quart fresh strawberries, hulled and halved*
     1   *tablespoon fructose*
     2   *teaspoons cornstarch*
   ¹/₂ *cup water*
 1 to 2 *drops red food color*
     4   *Crepes (page 89)*

1. Mix together fructose, cornstarch and water. Cook over medium heat until bubbly and thickened. Cool slightly.
2. Pour mixture over strawberries and mix carefully.
3. Place each Crepe on a serving dish. Fill with ¹/₄ of strawberry mixture placed on middle of each Crepe. Fold over each side of the Crepe. Turn over so the seam is down.
4. Garnish with a little strawberry filling over center of Crepe.

Makes 4 servings.

Each serving contains:
   162   *calories*
     6   *grams protein*
    31   *grams carbohydrate*
     2   *gram fat*
    54   *mg. sodium*
    46   *mg. cholesterol*
     4   *grams fiber*

         ADA Exchange Value
     1   *Starch*
     1   *Fruit*
         negligible fat calories.

Floating Island

Custard Sauce
- 1 ¹/₂ *cups 1% milk*
- 1 *tablespoon cornstarch*
- 1 *teaspoon pure orange extract*
- ¹/₂ *teaspoon orange rind*
- ¹/₂ *teaspoon pure vanilla extract*
- 2 *packets Equal*™

Meringue
- 4 *egg whites (room temperature)*
- ¹/₈ *teaspoon cream of tartar*
- ¹/₈ *cup fructose*
- 1 *10 ¹/₂ oz. can mandarin oranges packed in water
fresh mint to garnish*

Custard Sauce
1. Heat milk and cornstarch in sauce pan over medium heat until it comes to a boil. Remove from heat.
2. Stir in orange rind, extract, vanilla and Equal™. Chill.

Meringue
1. Beat egg whites with cream of tartar until foamy. Continue beating at high speed. Slowly add fructose until stiff peaks form when beater is slowly raised.
2. Spoon mixture into a 5-cup mold that has been sprayed with vegetable spray. Press down to remove air pockets.
3. Place mold in a baking pan with boiling water 2 inch deep and bake in a 350 degree oven for 25 minutes (or until knife inserted in center comes out clean).
4. Cool on a rack 5 minutes.
5. Spoon chilled custard into serving bowl. Loosen edge of mold with a spatula and unmold on custard.
6. Place orange slices around meringue. Garnish with fresh mint. Serve.

Makes 6 servings.

Each serving contains:
- *90 calories*
- *4 grams protein*
- *17 grams carbohydrate*
- *1 gram fat*
- *67 mg. sodium*
- *3 mg. cholesterol*
- *negligible grams fiber*

ADA Exchange Value
- *1/2 Starch*
- *1 Fruit*
- *negligible fat calories.*

Pears a la Cream

8   canned pear halves, packed in water
    Almond Cream (page 117), omitting
    chopped almonds

Place each pear half in a dessert dish. Spoon the Almond
Cream over each one. Chill until ready to serve.

Makes 8 servings.

Each serving contains:
  127   calories
    5   grams protein
   24   grams carbohydrates
    1   gram fat
   71   mg. sodium
    4   mg. cholesterol
    2   grams fiber

      ADA Exchange Value
  ¹/₂   Milk
    1   Fruit
   9%   of total calories are from fat.

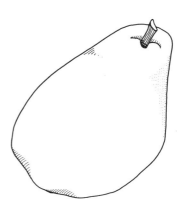

Almond Cream

1 1/2 **cups 1% milk**
3 **tablespoons cornstarch**
1 1/2 **teaspoons pure vanilla extract**
1 1/2 **teaspoons almond extract**
2 **packets Equal™**
2 **egg whites**
1/4 **teaspoon cream of tartar**
1 1/2 **teaspoons ground almonds**

1. Combine milk and cornstarch in medium sauce pan and cook over medium heat, stirring constantly until mixture comes to a boil and thickens. Remove from heat.
2. Stir in vanilla, almond extract and Equal™.
3. Beat egg whites until stiff. Fold into milk mixture.
4. Divide into 6 4-oz. dessert dishes and sprinkle each one with 1/4 teaspoon ground almonds.

Makes 6 servings.

Each serving contains:
58 **calories**
3 **grams protein**
7 **grams carbohydrate**
1 **gram fat**
48 **mg. sodium**
3 **mg. cholesterol**
negligible grams fiber

ADA Exchange Value
1/2 **Milk**
15% **of total calories are from fat.**

Section III
Mexican

About Mexican Food

Ever popular Mexican food is derived from both Spanish and Native American Indian influences. The cuisine uses staples such as corn, rice, beans, tomatoes and a host of flavorings including garlic, chilis of all varieties, cilantro and cumin. Various regions of the country influence the cooking and seasoning style, particularly in the Southwest where California, Arizona, New Mexico and Texas all border Mexico. We hear reference to Sonora style, Santa Fe style, Tex-Mex and California style. These are all regional variations in preparation, seasoning and serving style.

Mexican food is traditionally high in complex carbohydrate but cooking techniques often use lard or other fats. By limiting fats, Mexican food can add exciting variety, flavor and appeal to your food plan.

Mexican Fiesta

May 5th, "Cinco de Mayo," is the perfect time to have a
MEXICAN FIESTA

Decorate with bright colors and have mariachi music playing.
If you're having a big party, hire a live mariachi band.
A piñata filled with goodies adds a festive touch.

Start with a Margarita
Use a good quality gold tequila,
but use very little per drink—or have virgin Margaritas.

Appetizers
Oven Baked Tortilla Chips
Bean Dip
Guacamole
Three Cheese Layered Appetizer
Salsa

Serve Buffet Style
Jicama Salad
Tamales
Chicken Enchiladas
Bean and Mushroom Salad
Black Bean and Corn Relish

Dessert
Fresh Fruit
Mexican Coffee

MEXICAN LUNCHEON

Salad

Chili Rellano
Refried Beans
Spanish Rice

Flan

About Tortillas

Tortillas are the mainstay of Mexican food. They are eaten at virtually every meal. Corn tortillas are traditionally made with little or no fat and have fewer calories than flour tortillas—as long as they are eaten fresh off the griddle or steamed (in other words without fat added). Corn tortillas can be purchased fresh, frozen or canned, depending on what part of the country you live in. We recommend you try your hand at homemade tortillas once in a while, as they add a special flavor.

Flour tortillas are traditionally made with lard or other solid fat and are usually larger than corn tortillas — and therefore contain more calories. We have reduced the fat, eliminated the lard and pared down the size so these flour tortillas are more in line with corn tortillas.

Flour Tortillas

3 cups whole wheat flour
$1/2$ teaspoon baking powder
1 tablespoon corn oil margarine
1 to 1 $1/2$ cups boiling water

1. Melt margarine in $1/2$ cup boiling water.
2. Mix flour and baking powder.
3. Gradually mix water/margarine into flour until all flour is moistened and mixture forms a soft, non-sticky ball. Add more water if needed for proper consistency.
4. Shape into18 balls, each about the size of an egg.
5. Roll out tortillas with a rolling pin, turning clockwise $1/4$ turn each time you roll. They will gradually roll out into thin circles.
6. Heat a cast iron skillet or nonstick griddle to a medium/hot temperature.
7. Drop tortillas onto pan or griddle and cook 15 to 30 seconds each side, until they change from a dark to a slightly light color. Cool.
8. Wrap in plastic or foil and store in refrigerator. They can also be frozen. If tortillas dry out around the edges, or all over, steam them for 15 to 30 seconds and they'll become soft and pliable again. Tortillas will last in the refrigerator about two weeks.

Makes 18 tortillas. One serving = 1 tortilla

Each serving contains:
72 calories
3 grams protein
14 grams carbohydrate
1 gram fat
0 mg. cholesterol
17 mg. sodium
3 grams dietary fiber

ADA Exchange Value
1 Starch
13% of total calories are from fat.

Chicken Broth

1	**3 pound chicken**
3	**stalks celery**
2	**large carrots**
2	**cloves garlic**
$^1/_4$	**cup fresh parsley**
1	**large onion**
	all purpose herb seasoning
	water

1. Rinse chicken and place in a crock pot or large pot and cover with water.
2. Peel and chop vegetables into large chunks. Split garlic cloves in half.
3. Add vegetables, garlic and parsley to pot. Sprinkle in about 1 teaspoon herb seasoning.
4. Cover and bring to a boil. Then simmer several hours.
5. Strain broth into another pot and discard vegetables.
6. Remove skin and bones from chicken. Shred chicken meat into medium-sized pieces and refrigerate or freeze for use in other recipes.
7. Chill broth for several hours. Then remove layer of fat from top. Use broth for cooking rice or other dishes needing flavor without adding salt.

Makes about 8 cups. 1 serving = 1 cup

Each serving contains:

10	**calories**
	negligible grams protein
2	**grams carbohydrate**
	negligible grams fat
30	**mg. sodium**
0	**mg. cholesterol**
0	**grams fiber**

**ADA Exchange Value
negligible**

THE GUILTLESS GOURMET GOES ETHNIC

Barbara's Mexican-Style Chicken Soup

1	whole chicken, about 3 pounds
	water
1	teaspoon cumin seeds
1	bunch cilantro, washed
1 1/3	cups brown rice, cooked
2	fresh tomatoes, diced
4	thin slices avocado
1/2	cup Red Salsa (page 133), if desired

1. Rinse chicken thoroughly removing innards and extra fat. Place in a soup pot and cover with water. Add cumin seeds and entire bunch of cilantro. Bring to a boil. Then simmer until done, usually about 2 hours.
2. Remove chicken from broth and allow to cool slightly. Strain broth to remove cumin and cilantro. Then allow broth to chill and remove fat layer before using.
3. Meanwhile, remove meat from chicken bones. Then chill until ready to use.
4. To serve, reheat broth with chicken in it. Place 1/3 cup cooked brown rice into each of four soup dishes, ladle broth and chicken on top. Then garnish with diced tomatoes and a slice of avocado. Serve Salsa on the side if extra spiciness is desired.

Makes 4 servings.

Each serving contains:
- *267 calories*
- *29 grams protein*
- *26 grams carbohydrate*
- *6 grams fat*
- *79 mg. sodium*
- *66 mg. cholesterol*
- *4 grams fiber*

ADA Exchange Value
3   *Lean Meat*
1   *Starch*
1   *Vegetable*
21%   *of total calories are from fat.*

Albondigas
(Meatball Soup)

8 cups Chicken Broth (page 124)
2 carrots, peeled and sliced
2 zucchini squash, scrubbed and sliced
1/2 head cabbage, chopped coarsely
8 cobbettes of corn
1 pound raw ground turkey
1 slice bread, ground into crumbs
2 egg whites
1 teaspoon oregano leaves

1. Place Chicken Broth into a large pot. Bring to a simmer adding sliced carrots, zucchini and cabbage.
2. Mix raw turkey with bread crumbs. Stir in egg whites and oregano and mix thoroughly. Make into 16 meatballs.
3. Drop meatballs, one at a time, into soup allowing broth to return to a slow simmer.
4. Simmer soup about 15 minutes or until meatballs are cooked through.

Makes 8 servings.

Each serving contains:
161 calories
19 grams protein
17 grams carbohydrate
3 grams fat
756 mg. sodium
36 mg. cholesterol
4 grams fiber

ADA Exchange Value
2 Lean Meat
1 Starch
15% of total calories are from fat.

Lima Bean Soup

1 **pound dry baby lima beans, approx. 6 cups cooked**
1 **pound can whole tomatoes, no salt added**
1 **small onion, minced**
2 **teaspoons marjoram**
1/4 **teaspoon black pepper**
1 **cup carrots, sliced**
1 **cup celery, sliced**
8 **cups Chicken Broth (page 124)**

1. Place lima beans in a soup pot. Cover with boiling water and let sit for one hour. Drain off liquid.
2. Add 8 cups of Chicken Broth to beans. Break up tomatoes and add.
3. Spray a heavy skillet with nonstick spray and saute onion until tender. Add marjoram and stir to mix. Add this mixture to beans along with pepper, carrots and celery.
4. Simmer soup, partially covered, for about one hour or until beans are tender.

Makes 8 servings.

Each serving contains:
165 *calories*
10 *grams protein*
30 *grams carbohydrate*
1 *gram fat*
300 *mg. sodium*
1 *mg. cholesterol*
6 *grams fiber*

ADA Exchange Value
2 *Starch*
1/2 *Lean Meat*
7% *of total calories are from fat.*

Gaspacho

1 **clove garlic, minced**
¹/₂ **onion, minced**
2 **tablespoons green chili, roasted, peeled and chopped**
1 **pound can tomatoes, no salt added**
¹/₂ **cucumber, chopped**
2 **fresh tomatoes, chopped**
juice of ¹/₂ lime
dash of hot pepper sauce

1. Start food processor or blender. Carefully add garlic through the top opening. Add onion and roasted chili.
2. Stop food processor or blender. Add canned tomatoes and blend well.
3. Pour mixture into a bowl and stir in cucumber and fresh tomato.
4. Add lime juice and hot pepper sauce. Chill and serve as a cold soup for an appetizer or as a condiment.

Makes 4 generous servings.

Each serving contains:

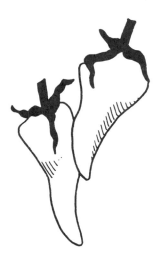

    35 *calories*
     2 *grams protein*
     8 *grams carbohydrate*
       negligible grams fat
   14 *mg. sodium*
     0 *mg. cholesterol*
     2 *grams fiber*

       ADA Exchange Value
1 ¹/₂ *Vegetable*
       negligible fat calories.

Three Layer Cheese Appetizer

1   *pound lowfat ricotta cheese*
4   *oz. lowfat cream cheese*
$^1/_2$ *cup onion, finely chopped*
1   *clove garlic, finely chopped*
2   *tablespoons pine nuts, toasted*
4   *oz. jar pimento, drained well and pureed*
$^1/_2$ *teaspoon ground cumin*
1   *tablespoon jalapeno pepper*
3   *tablespoons cilantro leaves, chopped*

1. Spray a heavy skillet with nonstick spray and saute onion and garlic until tender.
2. Using a blender or food processor, combine ricotta cheese and cream cheese until well blended. Add garlic and onion, mix well and divide into three small bowls.
3. To one bowl, mix in toasted pine nuts.
4. To another bowl, add pureed pimento mixed with cumin.
5. To last bowl, add jalapeno pepper and approx. 2 tablespoons chopped cilantro leaves.
6. Prepare a 5 to 6 cup mold by lining with plastic wrap or cheese cloth. Carefully spoon pine nut mixture into bottom of mold. Spoon pimento mixture on top and follow with pepper/ cilantro mixture.
7. Fold ends of plastic wrap or cheese cloth over top of mold and press down lightly to compact. Chill overnight.
8. To serve, invert mold onto a platter and carefully remove wrapping. Garnish with 1 tablespoon cilantro leaves.
9. Serve with raw vegetables or baked corn tortilla chips.

Makes 12 servings.

Each serving contains:
    78   calories
    6   grams protein
    4   grams carbohydrate
    5   grams fat

224 mg. sodium
 14 mg. cholesterol
  1 gram fiber

ADA Exchange Value
$^1/_2$ **Medium Fat Meat**
$^1/_2$ **Vegetable**
52% **of total calories are from fat.**

About Salsa

Salsa is a general term that means "a sauce." Salsa or "chili" is used as a condiment or ingredient in virtually all Mexican-style meals including breakfast. Salsas may be fresh (raw) or cooked and vary in spiciness from mild to very hot. Salsas are usually very low in calories and may be used as desired. Store bought salsas, although convenient, may be higher in salt or sodium. You can use a food processor, blender or chop all ingredients by hand. Salsas can be chunky or smooth. Make it whatever consistency you like.

Red Salsa

1   **pound Roma or Italian plum tomatoes**
$^1/_2$ **pound tomatoes**
$^1/_2$ **red Spanish onion**
2   **cloves garlic**
$^1/_2$ **cup loose packed fresh cilantro leaves**
1   **Serrano chili**
    juice of 1 lime
    sweetener, approx. $^1/_8$th of a teaspoon
$^1/_4$ **teaspoon chili powder, optional**

1. Cut stems off tomatoes and coarsely chop.
2. Peel onion and garlic and coarsely chop.
3. Remove stem and seeds from chili and chop.
4. In a food processor or blender, chop garlic, cilantro and chili pepper.
5. Add onions and chop.
6. Add tomatoes and chop to desired consistency — chunky or pureed.
7. Remove mixture to a bowl.
8. Add lime juice, sweetener and chili powder
9. Serve with baked tortilla chips or use as a sauce or a garnish for hot or cold foods.

Salsa is good on baked potatoes and makes a delicious oil-free salad dressing.

Makes 8 servings.

Each serving includes:
  29 **calories**
   1 **gram protein**
   7 **grams carbohydrate**
     negligible grams fat
  13 **mgs. sodium**

0 mg. cholesterol
2 grams fiber

ADA Exchange Value
1 Vegetable
negligible fat calories.

Black Bean and Corn Relish

2   cups cooked black beans, cooled to room temperature
1   cup fresh or frozen kernels of corn
1   recipe Red Salsa (page 133)

1. Combine beans and corn in a large bowl. Add Red Salsa and mix well.
2. Allow to marinate a few hours before serving.
3. Serve as side dish or wrapped in a tortilla.

Makes 8 servings.

Each serving contains:
- 83   *calories*
- 4   *grams protein*
- 17   *grams carbohydrate*
-    *negligible grams fat*
- 6   *mg. sodium*
- 0   *mg. cholesterol*
- 6   *grams fiber*

ADA Exchange Value
- 1   *Starch*
-    *negligible fat calories*

Guacamole

This is a very smooth dip or spread. If you would prefer a chunky version, don't blend in the food processor, just mix all the ingredients by hand.

> 1 *medium avocado*
> 1 *cup nonfat cottage cheese*
> 2 *tablespoons salsa*

1. Place cottage cheese in food processor with steel blade and blend until very smooth.
2. Cut avocado in half, remove seed and scoop meat into the processor with cottage cheese. Blend until smooth.
3. Add salsa and quickly blend.
4. Place into serving bowl. Cover and refrigerate until ready to eat.

Makes 6 servings.

Each serving contains:
> 86 *calories*
> 6 *grams protein*
> 5 *grams carbohydrate*
> 6 *grams fat*
> 159 *mg. sodium*
> 2 *mg. cholesterol*
> 1 *gram fiber*

> *ADA Exchange Value*
> 1 *Vegetable*
> 1 *Fat*
> 63% *of total calories are from fat.*

Ranchero Sauce

1   onion, peeled and cut into thin slices
1   medium tomato
1   clove garlic, minced
   Chicken Broth (page 124)
1   teaspoon flour

1. Spray a heavy skillet with nonstick spray and heat. Saute onion and garlic until soft but not brown.
2. Add tomato and cook a few minutes. Add about 4 tablespoons of Chicken Broth.
3. Cook until liquid is slightly reduced, then sprinkle 1 teaspoon flour on top of sauce and quickly blend in.
4. Simmer until desired consistency. Pour over Chili Rellenos and serve.

Makes 4 servings.

Each serving contains:
   23   calories
   1   gram protein
   5   grams carbohydrate
      negligible grams fat
   88   mg. sodium
      negligible mg. cholesterol
   1   gram fiber

   ADA Exchange Value
   1   Vegetable
      negligible fat calories.

Double Bean and Mushroom Salad

$1/2$ **pound fresh green beans, washed and trimmed**
1 **cup fresh, cooked garbanzo beans**
1 **cup fresh mushrooms, sliced**
$1/4$ **cup red onion, sliced into rings**
1 **medium tomato, sliced**

Dressing

1 **tablespoon oil**
2 **tablespoons red wine vinegar**
2 **tablespoons lemon juice**
$1/8$ **teaspoon pepper**
1 **tablespoon grainy mustard**

1. Steam green beans until crisp tender, then plunge into a bowl of ice water to stop cooking process and retain color.
2. After beans have cooled, drain well and place in a shallow bowl or serving dish. Add garbanzo beans, sliced mushrooms, onion and tomato.
3. Prepare dressing by combining oil, vinegar, lemon juice, pepper and mustard. Mix well and pour over vegetables. Allow to marinate at least one hour, chilled.
4. Serve on a bed of lettuce or arrange vegetables on individual serving plates.

Makes 6 servings.

Each serving contains:

89 **calories**
3 **grams protein**
14 **grams carbohydrate**
3 **grams fat**
128 **mg. sodium**
0 **mg. cholesterol**
3 **grams fiber**
    ADA Exchange Value
$1/2$ **Starch**
1 **Vegetable**
$1/2$ **Fat**
30% **of total calories are from fat.**

THE GUILTLESS GOURMET GOES ETHNIC

Jicama Salad

4 cups jicama, shredded or julienne cut
¼ cup lime juice
¼ to ½ teaspoon chili powder
1 clove garlic, pressed for juice only
1 to 2 tablespoons cilantro, chopped fine
dash of sweetener

1. Put shredded jicama into a bowl.
2. In another small bowl, combine lime juice, chili powder, garlic juice, cilantro and sweetener. Mix well.
3. Pour dressing over jicama and mix to combine.
4. Cover and let sit for several hours in refrigerator to marinate.
5. Serve as side dish, salad or as a garnish.

Makes 4 servings.

Each serving contains:
55 calories
1 gram protein
12 grams carbohydrate
0 grams fat
9 mg. sodium
0 mg. cholesterol
2 grams fiber

ADA Exchange Value
2 Vegetable
negligible fat calories.

Zucchini Boats — Mexican Style

4 medium-sized zucchini squash
2 cloves garlic, minced
1/4 cup onion, minced
2 tomatillos, hulled, washed and chopped
2 tablespoons pimento, diced
2 egg whites
2 corn tortillas
1/2 cup lowfat cheese

Sauce

2 fresh tomatoes
1 tablespoon roasted green chilis
1/8 teaspoon cumin

1. Wash zucchini and cut off ends. Cook in a steamer until tender (approx. 7 minutes). Immediately place in a bowl of ice water to stop cooking process and to retain color. When cool, remove from water and slice off top of each zucchini, lengthwise.
2. Remove pulp from zucchini, leaving a firm shell. Dice zucchini pulp and reserve.
3. Spray a skillet with nonstick spray and saute garlic and onion one minute. Add tomatillos and cook until tender. Stir in pimento. Remove from heat.
4. In a small bowl, combine egg whites and cheese. Mix thoroughly. Add to tomatillo mixture.
5. Slice corn tortillas into strips, then chop fine. Mix into tomatillo mixture along with reserved zucchini.
6. Fill zucchini shells with mixture and place in a shallow baking pan that has been sprayed with nonstick spray.
7. Bake at 350 degrees about 20 minutes. Serve with sauce.
8. Puree tomatoes in a blender, adding roasted pepper and cumin. Heat in a saucepan and simmer a few minutes. Spoon over zucchini boats as they are served.

Makes 4 servings.

Each serving contains:
- *88 calories*
- *8 grams protein*
- *13 grams carbohydrate*
- *1 gram fat*
- *161 mg. sodium*
- *2 mg. cholesterol*
- *3 grams fiber*

ADA Exchange Value
- *2 Vegetable*
- *¹/₂ Fat*
- *13% of total calories are from fat.*

About Quesadillas

Quesadillas are usually served open-faced or folded. Flour
tortillas are probably more traditional, but corn tortillas may be
used as well. Use your microwave oven, toaster oven or oven/
broiler. Just watch them carefully as the cheese melts quickly
and they can become overdone and hard.

Cheese is, of course, often the only ingredient used and is
high in fat. We recommend using fat-reduced cheeses, jack,
cheddar or a combination of both. Go easy on the cheese. Use
more salsa or other low-calorie additions mentioned in the
following recipes.

Quesadillas

4 Tortillas (page 123)
1 cup low-fat cheese, shredded

1. Preheat oven to 450 degrees.
2. Place tortillas on a cookie sheet and sprinkle with ¼ cup cheese each.
3. Bake in oven (or broil) just until cheese melts.
4. Serve open-faced or folded, plain or with assorted condiments. Serve whole or cut into wedges.

Suggested condiments:
    fresh salsa
    fresh chopped tomatoes
    fresh or imitation crab meat

Makes 4 servings.

Each serving equals:
* 108 calories*
*   7 grams protein*
* 14 grams carbohydrate*
*   3 grams fat*
* 83 mg. sodium*
*   8 mg. cholesterol*
*   3 grams fiber*

*   ADA Exchange Value*
*   1 Starch*
* ½ Lean Meat*
28% of total calories are from fat.

Mexican Pizza

> *4 Flour Tortillas (page 123)*
> *1 cup low-fat cheese, shredded*
> *4 oz. cooked ground meat or*
> *2 Guiltless Chorizo (page 165)*
> *1 small tomato, chopped*
> *¹/₂ onion, peeled and chopped*
> *1 tablespoon chopped olives, optional*
> *fresh cilantro*

1. Preheat oven to 450 degrees.
2. Place tortillas on a cookie sheet.
3. Evenly divide cheese, meat or chorizo, tomatoes, onions and olives (if desired).
4. Bake in oven approx. 4 to 5 minutes or until cheese is melted and bubbly.
5. Remove from oven and place on serving dish. Garnish with cilantro. Cut into wedges, if desired.

Makes 4 servings.

Each serving contains:
> *196 calories*
> *14 grams protein*
> *16 grams carbohydrate*
> *9 grams fat*
> *114 mg. sodium*
> *33 mg. cholesterol*
> *3 grams fiber*

> *ADA Exchange Value*
> *1 Starch*
> *1 Lean Meat*
> *1 Fat*
> *40% of total calories are from fat.*

Burritos

A finger food to be eaten out of hand. A great way to use leftovers.

> **4** *Flour Tortillas (page 123)*
> **1 ¹/₃** *cups Guiltless Refried Beans (page 150) OR*
> **8** *oz. cooked meat or chicken OR*
> **²/₃** *cup of beans plus 4 oz. cooked sirloin steak, trimmed, OR skinless chicken*
> *salsa*

1. Heat beans or meat until hot.
2. Heat tortillas, one at a time, on griddle or on top of stove (gas range).
3. Place ¹/₄ of hot beans or meat mixture onto tortilla.
4. Add salsa and fold or roll to resemble a large cigar.

NOTE: Try adding leftover potatoes or rice to beans or meat mixture.

Makes 4 servings.

Each Bean Burrito serving contains:

- **152** *calories*
- **8** *grams protein*
- **29** *grams carbohydrate*
- **1** *gram fat*
- **24** *mg. sodium*
- **0** *mg. cholesterol*
- **9** *grams fiber*

> *ADA Exchange Value*
> **2** *Starch*
> **8%** *of total calories are from fat.*

Each Beef and Bean Burrito serving contains:
- 172 calories
- 14 grams protein
- 22 grams carbohydrate
- 4 grams fat
- 40 mg. sodium
- 25 mg. cholesterol
- 6 grams fiber

ADA Exchange Value
- 1 Starch
- 2 Lean Meat
- 20% of total calories are from fat.

Each Beef Burrito serving contains:
- 192 calories
- 20 grams protein
- 14 grams carbohydrate
- 6 grams fat
- 55 mg. sodium
- 50 mg. cholesterol
- 3 grams fiber

ADA Exchange Value
- 1 Starch
- 2 Lean Meat
- 29% of total calories are from fat.

Spicy Potato Wedges

4   small potatoes, scrubbed well
nonstick spray
paprika
chili powder
¹/₄   cup chopped cilantro

1. Cut potatoes into wedges or strips and spread out on a cookie sheet. Spray potato wedges on all sides with nonstick spray.
2. Sprinkle paprika and chili powder over potatoes, being sure to coat all sides. Sprinkle with cilantro in the same manner.
3. Bake potato wedges in a 400 degree oven for 20 minutes or until fork tender. Serve hot or cold.

Makes 4 servings.

Each serving contains:
115   calories
3   grams protein
26   grams carbohydrate
negligible grams fat
12   mg. sodium
0   mg. cholesterol
2   grams fiber

ADA Exchange Value
1 ¹/₂   Starch
negligible fat calories.

About Beans

Dried, cooked beans are another staple of Mexican-style cookery. Pinto beans, kidney beans or black beans are generally used. Beans are high in complex carbohydrate and are an excellent source of protein, fiber and trace minerals. Beans are often considered to be high in calories, but often the high calories are a result of added ingredients such as fat. Without added fat, beans are healthy and nutritious and very inexpensive. We recommend cooking beans ahead and storing them in the freezer in one or two cup containers. Canned beans can be used but will usually be much higher in salt content and often have a different texture. Dried beans are very inexpensive and are available all year round. Look for them in the rice and pasta section of your grocery store.

Basic Beans

*1 pound dried beans such as pinto, kidney,
garbanzo or black beans*
water
broth
onion
celery
garlic

1. Place beans in a strainer or sieve and rinse under running water.
2. Place beans in a large bowl and cover with water.
3. Let beans soak for 6 to 8 hours or overnight.
4. Drain beans and place in a large pot.
5. Cover with fresh water or broth.
6. Chop onion and 2 to 3 stalks of celery into large chunks. Peel garlic and cut in half. Add to pot of beans.
7. Bring beans to a boil. Reduce to simmer and cook until done. Time will vary according to type of bean.
8. Cool slightly and divide beans and liquid into freezer containers.
9. Store in freezer until needed. Use within 3 to 4 months.

Makes 10 servings.

Each serving contains:
   158 calories
   9 grams protein
   30 grams carbohydrate
   1 gram fat
   13 mg. sodium
   0 mg. cholesterol
   12 grams fiber

   ADA Exchange Value
   2 Starch
   1/2 Lean Meat
   4% of total calories are from fat.

Guiltless Refried Beans

2 cups cooked pinto beans, including bean juice
¹/₂ teaspoon chili powder

1. Spray a heavy skillet with nonstick spray and heat.
2. Add beans and juice, mashing and stirring beans until desired consistency.
3. Add chili powder and stir to mix.

Makes 6 servings.

Each serving contains:
- *80 calories*
- *5 grams protein*
- *15 grams carbohydrate*
- *negligible grams fat*
- *7 mg. sodium*
- *0 mg. cholesterol*
- *6 grams fiber*

ADA Exchange Value
1 Starch/Bread
negligible fat calories.

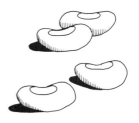

Mexican Rice

2 tomatoes, chopped into large chunks
$1/2$ onion, chopped into large chunks
2 cloves garlic, peeled and cut in half
1 cup brown rice
1 tablespoon corn oil
$1/4$ teaspoon chili powder
small bunch of cilantro
$1 1/2$ cups Chicken Broth (page 124) or water

1. Combine tomatoes, onion and garlic in a blender and puree.
2. Strain mixture into a small bowl and add chili powder.
3. Heat oil in a heavy pan or skillet.
4. Brown the rice in hot oil stirring constantly so it will not burn.
5. When rice is browned, add tomato mixture and broth or water.
6. Place bunch of cilantro on top of rice — do not stir in.
7. Bring to a boil, then reduce heat to simmer
8. Cover and cook approx. 45 minutes or until rice is done and all liquid is absorbed.
9. Carefully remove cilantro. Stir slightly and serve.

Makes 5 servings. 1 serving = $1/3$ cup

Each serving contains:
87 calories
2 grams protein
13 grams carbohydrate
4 grams fat
418 mg. sodium
negligible mg. cholesterol
2 grams fiber

ADA Exchange Value
1 Starch
$1/2$ Fat
14% of total calories are from fat.

Mexican-Style Corn Bread

  2 *egg whites*
 ³/₄ *cup 1% milk*
  2 *tablespoons oil*
  1 *tablespoon pimento, chopped*
1 to 2 *chilis, roasted and chopped (about ¹/₂ cup)*
  1 *cup frozen corn kernels, thawed*
  1 *cup low-fat cheddar cheese (4 oz.)*
  1 *cup cornmeal*
  1 *cup flour*
  4 *teaspoons baking powder*

1. Combine egg white, milk and oil. Stir in pimento and chopped chilis.
2. Combine cornmeal, flour and baking powder. Stir in cheese and corn kernels.
3. Add liquid ingredients and beat about one minute.
4. Spread evenly in a 9x9x2 inch baking dish that has been sprayed with nonstick spray.
5. Bake at 400 degrees 35 to 40 minutes. Cool and cut into 12 servings.

Makes 12 servings.

Each serving contains:
 149 *calories*
   5 *grams protein*
  23 *grams carbohydrate*
   5 *grams fat*
 181 *mg. sodium*
   6 *mg. cholesterol*
   2 *grams fiber*

     ADA Exchange Value
 1¹/₂ *Starch*
   1 *Fat*
 27% *of total calories are from fat.*

Chili Puree

1   package of dried chilis, milder variety preferred
water

1. Rinse chilis thoroughly under running water and place in a pot.
2. Cover with water. Bring to a boil. Turn off heat. Cover and let sit for about 20 minutes.
3. Let chilis cool to a point you can handle them. Remove stems and seeds and place pulp in a blender.
4. Add a small amount of water chilis were cooked in and blend to a puree.

This puree is the basis for enchilada sauces and many other seasonings. Store in the refrigerator tightly covered.

Makes 6 servings.

Each serving contains:
5   calories
negligible grams protein
1   gram carbohydrate
negligible grams fat
5   mg. sodium
0   mg. cholesterol
negligible grams fiber

ADA Exchange Value
negligible
negligible fat calories.

Enchilada Sauce

 1 **pound can tomatoes, no added salt**
 ¹/₄ to ¹/₂ **cup chili puree**
 2 **cloves garlic, minced**
 ¹/₂ **teaspoon cumin**
 ¹/₂ **teaspoon oregano**

1. Puree tomatoes in a blender
2. Add chili puree to tomatoes and blend.
3. Spray a heavy skillet with nonstick spray. Saute garlic until tender and lightly browned.
4. Add tomato/chili puree to pan and stir in cumin and oregano.
5. Simmer for a few minutes. If consistency is too thick, add a few tablespoons of water or broth.

Makes about 2 cups. Makes 6 servings.

Each serving contains:
 23 **calories**
 1 **gram protein**
 5 **grams carbohydrate**
 negligible grams fat
 135 **mg. sodium**
 0 **mg. cholesterol**
 2 **grams fiber**

 ADA Exchange Value
 1 **Vegetable**
 negligible fat calories.

Quick Enchilada Sauce

1 cup Chicken Broth (page 124)
1 cup tomato sauce, no salt added preferred
1 tablespoon tomato paste
1 tablespoon chili powder
2 cloves garlic, pressed
$^1/_2$ teaspoon oregano
$^1/_4$ teaspoon cumin

1. Combine all ingredients in a sauce pan.
2. Bring to a boil, then reduce to simmer for about 20 minutes.

Makes about 2 cups. 1 serving = $^1/_2$ cup.

Each serving contains:
        36 calories
         2 grams protein
         8 grams carbohydrate
           negligible grams fat
       296 mg. sodium
         0 mg. cholesterol
         3 grams fiber

        ADA Exchange Value
         1 Vegetable
           negligible calories are from fat

Chicken Enchiladas

12 corn tortillas
6 oz. cooked chicken, shredded or diced
6 oz. lowfat jack or cheddar cheese, reserve a little
  for top of casserole
1/2 onion, chopped fine
  cilantro leaves
2 cups Enchilada Sauce (page 154)

1. Heat Enchilada Sauce in a skillet until hot.
2. Dip a tortilla into sauce, then remove to a clean, flat surface.
3. Place 1/2 oz. each chicken and cheese in middle of tortilla and top with a sprinkle of minced onion. Fold tortilla into thirds and place seam side down into a baking dish large enough to hold the full dozen.
4. Repeat this process until all tortillas are stuffed.
5. Spoon remaining Enchilada Sauce over tortillas. Top with a little reserved cheese. Cover and bake at 350 degrees approx. 30 minutes or until hot and bubbly.

Makes 6 servings.

Each serving contains:
253 calories
19 grams protein
19 grams carbohydrate
12 grams fat
215 mg. sodium
22 mg. cholesterol
3 grams fiber

ADA Exchange Value
1 Starch
2 Lean Meat
1 Fat
41% of total calories are from fat.

Chili Rellenos

8   *large fresh green chilis*
8   *oz. low-fat jack cheese*
4   *egg whites*
2   *tablespoons flour*

1. Roast chilis over an open flame on a gas range or in the broiler. Chilis should be very blackened and skin bubbly.
2. Place chilis in a paper bag or dish cloth to steam for a few minutes. Then carefully scrape off blackened skin.
3. Make a slit lengthwise into each chili and carefully remove seeds.
4. Cut cheese into 8 equal long pieces and place each cheese stick into chili being careful not to tear the chili.
5. Whip egg whites until very frothy. Then whip in 2 tablespoons of flour.
6. Dip each cheese-stuffed chili into egg mixture and roll to cover thoroughly.
7. Place chilis in a baking dish and bake at 375 degrees for about 30 minutes or until egg mixture has browned and cheese is melted. Remove to a serving plate and top with Ranchero Sauce (page 137).

Makes 4 servings.

Each serving contains:
202   *calories*
18   *grams protein*
11   *grams carbohydrate*
10   *grams fat*
317   *mg. sodium*
32   *mg. cholesterol*
2   *grams fiber*

ADA Exchange Value
2   *Vegetable*
2 1/2   *Lean Meat*
1/2   *Fat*
42%   *of total calories are from fat.*

Fajitas

1 pound lean chicken or beef
1/2 cup lime or lemon juice
2 tablespoons low sodium soy sauce
2 tablespoons water
2 tablespoons tequila (optional)
1/2 teaspoon oregano
1/4 teaspoon cumin
1 clove garlic, crushed
1 small onion, thinly sliced
1 green pepper, remove stem, seeds and slice thinly
1 red or yellow pepper, remove stem, seeds and slice thinly
  nonstick spray
8 tortillas
  salsa
  cilantro

1. Cut lean beef or chicken into chunks or strips and place in a glass dish.
2. Combine lime or lemon juice, soy sauce, water, tequila, oregano, cumin and garlic juice in a small bowl.
3. Pour mixture over beef or chicken. Add sliced onions and stir to mix.
4. Cover and marinate in refrigerator no more than 4 hours for chicken, longer for beef, if desired.
5. Spray a heavy skillet with nonstick spray and heat.
6. Drain beef or chicken and add to skillet. Add sliced peppers and cook mixture just until meat is done and peppers are soft.
7. Divide mixture into 4 serving dishes such as au gratin dishes.
8. Serve with tortillas, salsa and cilantro.

Makes 4 servings.

Each Chicken Fajita serving contains:
- 368 *calories*
- 39 *grams protein*
- 41 *grams carbohydrate*
- 7 *grams fat*
- 338 *mg. sodium*
- 88 *mg. cholesterol*
- 7 *grams fiber*

ADA Exchange Value
- 2 *Starch*
- 2 *Vegetable*
- 3 *Lean Meat*
- 16% *of total calories are from fat.*

Each Beef Fajita serving contains:
- 408 *calories*
- 42 *grams protein*
- 41 *grams carbohydrate*
- 10 *grams fat*
- 334 *mg. sodium*
- 96 *mg. cholesterol*
- 7 *grams fiber*

ADA Exchange Value
- 2 *Starch*
- 2 *Vegetable*
- 3 *Lean Meat*
- 1 *Fat*
- 21% *of total calories are from fat.*

About Tamales

Tamales are a time-consuming food to prepare but are well worth the effort. Traditional tamales are made with lard, which contains cholesterol and saturated fat. Fillings can be high in calories as well, but the pork loin used in the following recipe is quite lean. Traditional tamales are also made with beef or chicken fillings and in some cases, fruit.

Corn husks are usually available in grocery stores, especially around the holidays. Specialty stores or Mexican delis usually carry them as well.

Assembling Pork Tamales

You will need approximately 30 corn husks, soaked in water until soft and pliable. Place each husk on a flat surface with smaller end facing away from you. Spray the surface with nonstick spray. Take about 1 1/2 to 2 tablespoons Masa Dough and place in center of corn husk. Using dampened fingers, press the dough out towards edges of husk. Place about 1 tablespoon of pork filling on dough. Fold top end of husk over filling. Then fold the left, then right side to the middle making a small and compact package. Continue making tamales until ingredients are gone.

Place tamales in a steamer (they may be piled on top of each other) and steam for 45 to 60 minutes. Cool tamales, then package to store. They freeze well or can be refrigerated for a few days.

To serve tamales, steam to reheat on top of the stove or in a microwave oven.

Makes 27 tamales.

Masa For Tamales

    4   cups Masa Harina (corn meal, available at
        grocery stores)
  1/4   cup oil
3 1/2 to 4   cups Chicken Broth (page 124)

1. Using a heavy mixer, combine Masa Harina and oil. Mix until very crumbly.
2. Slowly add chicken mixing to desired consistency of a dough that will hold together but is not too sticky.
3. Cover dough with a damp cloth and keep damp until ready to use.

Makes 27 servings.

Pork For Tamales

1 ⅓ **pounds fresh pork loin**
  3 **cloves garlic, minced**
  1 **medium onion, diced**
  6 **oz. tomato paste, no salt added**
12 **oz. water**
 ¼ **cup Chili Puree (page 153)**

1. Trim any visible fat off pork loin and cube into small, bite-sized pieces.
2. Spray a heavy skillet with nonstick spray and saute onions and garlic until browned.
3. Add pork loin cubes and cook until well browned.
4. Add tomato paste, water and Chili Puree. Stir to mix well.
5. Cover and cook 30 minutes until meat is very tender.

This mixture will fill approx. 27 tamales.

Each serving contains:
 136 **calories**
   8 **grams protein**
 15 **grams carbohydrate**
   5 **grams fat**
 196 **mg. sodium**
 17 **mg. cholesterol**
  1 **gram fiber**

    ADA Exchange Value
  1 **Starch**
  1 **Medium Fat Meat**
35% **of total calories are from fat.**

Mexican Lentil Soup

1 *pound lentils (6 to 7 cups cooked)*
2 *bay leaves*
6 *garlic cloves, roasted*
1 *medium red onion, chopped*
2 *large carrots, peeled and chopped*
2 *teaspoons cumin*
1 *teaspoon oregano*
1/4 *cup chili puree*
1 *tomato, chopped*
6 *cups Chicken Broth (page 124)*
  cilantro
  lime juice

1. Wash or rinse lentils and drain. Place in a large pot and cover with cold water. Add bay leaves and bring to a boil. Reduce heat and simmer until tender, approx. 30 minutes. Remove bay leaves.
2. Cut tops off each of the 6 garlic cloves. Place on a piece of foil or in a small oven-proof dish. Spray lightly with nonstick spray and place in a 325 degree oven to roast until tender, approx. 30 minutes. Remove from oven and let cool.
3. Squeeze garlic out of husks into a blender. Add chopped tomato and puree until smooth.
4. Spray a skillet with nonstick spray and saute diced onions and carrots until tender.
5. Add tomato/garlic puree and cooked vegetables to lentils. Add Chicken Broth.
6. Simmer soup for about 30 minutes.
7. Serve soup with sprigs of cilantro and squeeze of fresh lime juice.

Makes 12 servings.

Each serving contains:

- 145 calories
- 10 grams protein
- 26 grams carbohydrate
- 1 gram fat
- 300 mg. sodium
- negligible mg. cholesterol
- 5 grams fiber

ADA Exchange Value

- 1 1/2 Starch
- 1/2 Lean Meat
- 5% of total calories are from fat.

Guiltless Chorizo

>   1   **pound lean ground turkey**
>   1   **tablespoon chili powder**
> 2 to 3 **cloves garlic, crushed**
> 1 to 2 **tablespoons tequila (optional)**
>   1   **teaspoon oregano**
>   ½   **teaspoon cumin**
>   2   **egg whites**
>   **nonstick spray**
>   1   **tablespoon oil**

1. Combine ground turkey, chili powder, garlic, tequila, oregano, cumin and egg whites.
2. Mix thoroughly.
3. Shape into 12 meatballs or sausages.
4. Spray a heavy skillet with nonstick spray. Add oil and heat.
5. Brown chorizo — a few at a time — until done.
6. Use for any dish calling for chorizo or a spicy type of sausage. They will keep in the refrigerator 3 to 5 days if fully cooked.

Makes 12 sausages. 1 serving = 2 chorizo

Each serving contains:
>   123 **calories**
>   18 **grams protein**
>   2 **grams carbohydrate**
>   4 **grams fat**
>   66 **mg. sodium**
>   40 **mg. cholesterol**
>   **negligible grams fiber**
>
>   **ADA Exchange Value**
>   2 **Lean Meat**
>   5% **of total calories are from fat.**

Papaya Sherbet

1 *ripe papaya, peeled and cut into chunks*
1 *cup plain nonfat yogurt*
$^1/_2$ *teaspoon vanilla*
2 *tablespoons fructose*
$^1/_4$ *teaspoon cinnamon*

1. Put all ingredients into a blender and blend to mix well.
2. Pour mixture into a freezer-proof dish. Place into freezer.
3. Check and stir sherbet about every 30 minutes until evenly frozen. Cover.
4. Before serving, let sherbet stand at room temperature about 20 minutes. Stir slightly and scoop into chilled dessert dishes. Garnish with fresh mint.

Makes 4 servings.

Each serving contains:
84 *calories*
4 *grams protein*
16 *grams carbohydrate*
negligible grams fat
50 *mg. sodium*
0 *mg. cholesterol*
1 *gram fiber*

ADA Exchange Value
1 *Fruit*
$^1/_2$ *Lean Meat*
negligible fat calories.

Baked Grapefruit

2 grapefruit
2 tablespoons orange juice, fresh preferred
1 tablespoon fructose
2 teaspoons tequila (optional)
$1/4$ teaspoon cinnamon

1. Preheat oven to 475 degrees or broiler.
2. Cut each grapefruit in half. Section each half, then place in a heat-proof dish.
3. Spoon equally over grapefruit halves.
4. Bake in a very hot oven approximately 10 minutes or broil about 4 minutes until bubbly.

Makes 4 servings.

Each serving contains:
48 calories
negligible grams protein
11 grams carbohydrate
negligible grams fat
negligible mg. sodium
0 mg. cholesterol
1 gram fiber

ADA Exchange Value
1 Fruit
negligible fat calories

Section IV
Spanish

Spanish Cooking

Spanish cooking is reminiscent of bullfights, flamingo dancing and, of course, the painting of Goya. The Spaniards are great snackers, with their main meal eaten between 2 and 3 in the afternoon and dinner between 9 and 10. This makes it easy to understand the Spanish siesta!

There are some similarities to Mexican and Spanish cuisine. The main difference is that Spanish cooking has a French influence and is more delicate in flavor than Mexican. Spanish cooks use slow simmering methods, often using in clay pots. They use simple spices—thyme, bay leaf, cayenne, paprika, parsley and saffron—in moderation.

Spanish Dinner Party

Company for dinner with a Spanish flair.

Have flamingo music playing.

Use bright colored paper plates and napkins.

Appetizers

Crudities

Tossed Green Salad

Paella

Strawberry Sorbet

Tequila Marinated Shrimp

1 **pound medium to large shrimp, cooked**
1 **tablespoon olive oil**
$^1/_4$ **cup tequila**
$^1/_4$ **cup lime juice**
$^1/_4$ **teaspoon paprika**
$^1/_4$ **teaspoon chili powder**
1 **clove garlic, crushed**

1. Place cooked and shelled shrimp into a large glass bowl.
2. Combine rest of ingredients and pour over shrimp.
3. Cover and chill for several hours or overnight.

This marinated shrimp can be used as an appetizer on a toothpick, a first course or salad or as a cold main dish.

Makes 6 servings.

Each serving contains:
  143 *calories*
   18 *grams protein*
    4 *grams carbohydrate*
    4 *grams fat*
  135 *mg. sodium*
  133 *mg. cholesterol*
      negligible grams fiber

      ADA Exchange Value
    2 *Lean Meat*
    1 *Fat*
  25% *of total calories are from fat.*

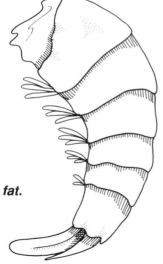

Spanish Rice

1 tablespoon olive oil
1 medium onion, chopped
2 cloves garlic, chopped
1 green bell pepper, chopped
1 medium tomato, peeled and chopped
$1/2$ teaspoon cayenne pepper
1 cup brown rice
$2 1/2$ cups Chicken Broth (page 124)

1. Heat olive oil in Dutch oven. Saute onion, garlic and bell pepper until soft.
2. Add tomato, cayenne pepper, and rice and stir. Add Chicken Broth and bring to a boil.
3. Reduce heat to simmer. Cover and cook 45 minutes or put in a 350 degree oven for 45 minutes.

Makes 4 servings.

Each serving contains:
113 *calories*
3 *grams protein*
17 *grams carbohydrate*
5 *grams fat*
101 *mg. sodium*
negligible mg. cholesterol
2 *grams fiber*

ADA Exchange Value
1 *Starch*
1 *Fat*
36% *of total calories are from fat.*

Spanish Salad

This is a good summer salad or side dish.

> 4 cups cooked brown rice
> 6 red, green and/or yellow bell peppers, roasted, peeled and cut in strips (see Tips)
> 2 red onions, cut in half, then sliced thin
> 6 tomatoes, peel and cut each into 8 segments (see Tips)
> 4 oz. can sliced green olives, drained
> 3/4 cup of Vinaigrette Dressing (page 29)
> fresh ground black pepper

1. Put rice on the bottom of serving dish. Arrange peppers, onion, tomatoes and olives on top.
2. Pour dressing over top and sprinkle with fresh ground pepper.

Makes 8 servings.

Each serving contains:
> 182 calories
> 4 grams
> 35 grams carbohydrate
> 4 grams fat
> 115 mg. sodium
> 0 mg. cholesterol
> 3 grams fiber
>
> ADA Exchange Value
> 1 Starch
> 2 Vegetable
> 1 Fat
> 18% of total calories are from fat.

Paella

This is a wonderful dish to serve to company. It is a very pretty one-dish meal.

 8 oz. *raw chicken breasts, boned and skinned*
 1 *tablespoon oil*
 6 *pieces Guiltless Chorizo (page 165), cooked*
 1 *onion, chopped*
 1 *clove garlic, minced*
 1 *teaspoon paprika*
 2 *tablespoons fresh parsley, chopped*
 $^1/_4$ *teaspoon pepper*
 1 *cup salt-free tomato juice*
 1 *cup lite beer (optional)*
   or use 1 cup Chicken Broth (page 124)
 1 *cup brown rice, uncooked*
 2 *tablespoons pimento, sliced*
 1 *9 oz. package frozen artichoke hearts, thawed*
 $^1/_2$ *pound large shrimp, cooked*
   or 6 fresh clams or mussels in shells
 1 *cup fresh or frozen peas*

1. Cut chicken into chunks or strips and brown in 1 tablespoon oil.
2. Add Chorizo and heat. Remove chicken and Chorizo from skillet and saute onion and garlic until lightly browned.
3. Add paprika, parsley, pepper, tomato juice and beer. Bring to a boil.
4. Add rice and pimento. Cover and simmer about 45 minutes or until rice is done and most of the liquid is absorbed.
5. Add chicken pieces, Chorizo, artichoke hearts, shrimp and sprinkle peas over the top. Cover and simmer about 10 minutes or until artichokes are tender and other ingredients are heated through.

Makes 6 servings.

Each serving contains:
- *285   calories*
- *33   grams protein*
- *20   grams carbohydrate*
- *7   grams fat*
- *176   mg. sodium*
- *116   mg. cholesterol*
- *4   grams fiber*

ADA Exchange Value
- *4   Lean Meat*
- *1   Starch*
- *1   Vegetable*
- *23%   of total calories are from fat.*

Spanish Pork

1 *pound lean pork shoulder, cut into 1 inch cubes*
2 *garlic cloves, chopped*
1 *small onion, chopped*
1 *28 oz. can whole peeled tomatoes, drained (reserve liquid)*
3 *green bell peppers, seeded, cut in half and sliced thin*
1/2 *teaspoon saffron*
2 *tablespoons fresh chopped parsley*
2 *cups short grain brown rice, uncooked*
5 *cups water*
2 *chicken bouillon cubes, low sodium*
fresh ground pepper

1. Heat a large Dutch oven. Then spray with a nonstick spray. Brown pork cubes on all sides. Remove from pan and set aside.
2. Add garlic, onion, tomatoes, and pepper to Dutch oven. Add quickly, saute, stirring constantly.
3. Add saffron, parsley and pork to Dutch oven and 1 cup of the water. Cover and simmer 20 minutes.
4. Stir in the rice and add 4 cups water along with the reserved juice from the tomatoes and chicken bouillon cubes. Cover and place in a preheated oven at 350 degrees for 1 1/2 hours.

Serve with a tossed green salad.

Makes 6 servings.

Each serving contains:
317 *calories*
28 *grams protein*
24 *grams carbohydrate*
12 *grams fat*

287 mg. sodium
80 mg. cholesterol
4 grams fiber

ADA Exchange Value
3 Lean Meat
1 Starch
1 Vegetable
1 Fat
34% of total calories are from fat.

Baked Spanish Halibut

3   *white onions, cut in half, sliced very thin*
2   *pounds of halibut*
¹/₂ *teaspoon fresh black ground pepper*
1   *garlic clove, minced*
1   *cup dry white wine*
2   *tomatoes, peeled and sliced (see Tips)*
2   *bay leaves*
4   *undercooked potatoes, sliced*

1. In an oven-proof serving dish sprayed with a nonstick spray, layer ¹/₂ of the onions.
2. Place fish on top and cover with pepper, garlic and wine.
3. Cover with remaining onions, tomatoes and bay leaves.
4. Place potatoes around fish.
5. Bake at 400 degrees for 45 minutes or until fish is done. Baste occasionally with cooking juices.

Makes 6 servings.

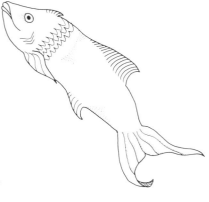

Each serving contains:
   287 *calories*
    33 *grams protein*
    23 *grams carbohydrate*
     4 *grams fat*
    93 *mg. sodium*
    48 *mg. cholesterol*
     3 *grams fiber*

       ADA Exchange Value
     4 *Lean Meat*
     1 *Starch*
     1 *Vegetable*
  11% *of total calories are from fat.*

Spanish Chicken

1   tablespoon olive oil
1   garlic clove, peeled
4   4 oz. chicken breasts, boned and skinned
¹/₂ teaspoon fresh ground black pepper
1   medium onion, chopped
2   bell peppers, seeded and chopped (red, green and/or yellow)
1   tablespoon paprika
¹/₄ teaspoon saffron
1   15 oz. can diced tomatoes
¹/₂ teaspoon cayenne pepper

1. Heat olive oil in large skillet. Saute garlic until golden brown. Then discard.
2. Add chicken breasts and brown on both sides. Sprinkle with pepper. Remove from skillet and set aside.
3. Add onions and peppers to skillet and saute until soft.
4. Add paprika, saffron, tomatoes and cayenne and mix together.
5. Place chicken back in pan. Cover and cook on low until chicken is done (about 20 minutes).

Makes 4 servings.

Each serving contains:

214 calories
27 grams protein
11 grams carbohydrate
8 grams fat
252 mg. sodium
66 mg. cholesterol
3 grams fiber

ADA Exchange Value

3 Lean Meat
2 Vegetables
32% of total calories are from fat.

Strawberry Sorbet

1   *20-oz. bag frozen strawberries, no sugar added*
3   *tablespoons fructose*

Put strawberries and fructose in food processor with steel blade and blend until mixture turns into strawberry ice. Serve immediately or store in freezer until ready to serve.

Makes 6 servings.

Each serving contains:
    39   calories
         negligible grams protein
     9   grams carbohydrate
         negligible grams fat
     8   mg. sodium
     0   mg. cholesterol
     1   gram fiber

         ADA Exchange Value
   ³/₄   Fruit
         negligible fat calories.

Orange Frappe

4 oranges, peeled
1/2 cup 1% milk
1 envelope unflavored gelatin
4 orange slices

1. Section oranges into a bowl removing membranes.
2. Drain the accumulated juice into a small saucepan.
3. Sprinkle gelatin over top of juice and let sit for one minute.
4. Heat juice and gelatin mixture and cook until gelatin is dissolved, about 4 to 5 minutes. Set aside to cool.
5. Place orange sections into a blender and blend to liquify. Gradually pour in milk while blending, then blend in cooled gelatin mixture in same manner.
6. Pour into 4 one-half cup dessert dishes. Chill. Garnish with mint leaves and a slice of orange.

Makes 4 servings.

Each serving contains:
81 calories
4 grams protein
17 grams carbohydrate
negligible grams fat
17 mg. sodium
1 mg. cholesterol
4 grams fiber

ADA Exchange Value
1 Fruit
1/2 Lean Meat
negligible fat calories

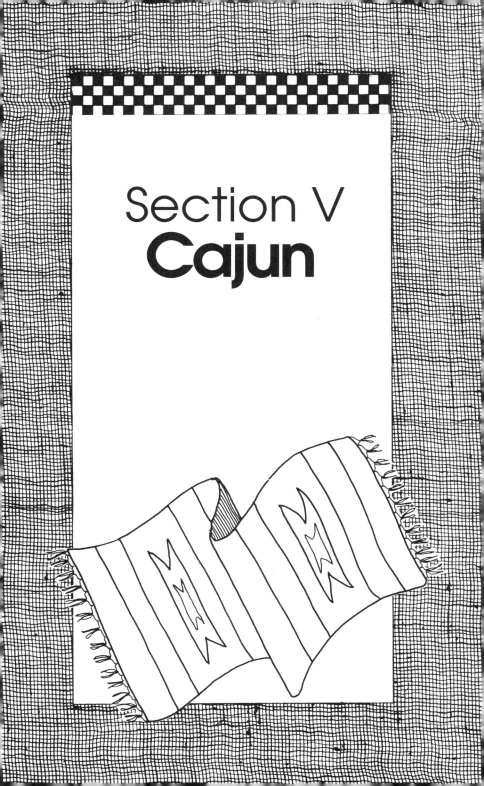

Section V
Cajun

Cajun

Cajun and Creole cooking are interesting combinations of French and Spanish cuisine with added influence from Choctaw Indians. We find Cajun and Creole cooking in Louisiana. In recent years we have seen the popularity grow throughout the USA. Cajun food preparation can be high in fat and sodium. However, this style is easy to modify by eliminating the high fat meats and the heavy use of butter and oils. Cajun uses lots of fresh ingredients and spices that are full of flavor, so it's easy to create very tasty dishes low in fats and salt. Spices found in the Cajun kitchen are peppers — black, white and red (cayenne)—powdered sassafras, parsley, bay leaf, Tabasco, garlic (fresh and powder), and onion powder.

CAJUN

The Cajun version of the all American barbeque.

Start your party in the late afternoon
on your patio with Dixieland Jazz
playing in the background.

Serve

Iced tea with fresh mint

Crudities and green onion dip

Mugs of corn chowder

Then in the dining room
change your music to a light jazz.

Serve

Jambalaya Salad

Cajun Oven Fried Chicken

Creole Corn

Dessert
Bananas Foster
Coffee

Green Onion Dip

8   ounces Yogurt Cheese (page 214)
1   tablespoon brown mustard
2   green onions, chopped fine
1/8   teaspoon cayenne pepper

Mix all ingredients together. Place in a covered container and place in the refrigerator at least 2 hours before serving. (It is better if made the day before serving.)

Makes 8 ounces.

Each serving contains:
225   calories
24   grams protein
32   grams carbohydrate
        negligible grams fat
150   mg. sodium
0   mg. cholesterol
0   grams fiber

        ADA Exchange Value
2   Nonfat Milk
        negligible fat calories.

Corn Chowder

1 cup celery, 1 to 2 stalks, chopped
1 onion, chopped
$^1/_4$ cup red pepper, chopped
2 small potatoes, peeled and diced
2 cups whole kernel corn
3 cups 1% milk

1. Spray a large pot with nonstick spray. Saute celery, onion, pepper and potato until softened but not browned.
2. Add corn and milk. Simmer, do not allow to boil, for about 35 minutes or until potatoes are cooked.
3. Remove about 2 cups of soup and put it into a blender. Blend until pureed. Then pour back into soup and stir. Reheat gently, remembering not to allow this soup to boil.

Makes 6 servings.

Each serving contains:

136	calories
6	grams protein
25	grams carbohydrate
2	grams fat
249	mg. sodium
5	mg. cholesterol
4	grams fiber

ADA Exchange Value

1$^1/_2$	Starch
1	Vegetable
13%	of total calories are from fat.

Black Bean Soup

2   cups black beans (soaked 8 hours)
    water
2   medium onions, coarsely chopped
2   cloves garlic, chopped
2   carrots, coarsely chopped
4   stalks celery, coarsely chopped
1   tablespoon cumin
2   bay leaves
2   tablespoons fresh parsley, chopped
1   teaspoon fresh ground pepper
1/2 cup dry sherry (optional)

1. Place beans in a large pot and cover with water. Bring to a boil. Reduce heat, cover and simmer for one hour removing any froth or foam.
2. Spray a skillet with nonstick spray. Saute onions about 4 minutes. Add garlic, carrots, celery and cumin. Saute until vegetables are soft or tender.
3. Add bay leaves, parsley, pepper. Mix well and add whole mixture to beans. Add sherry, if desired.
4. Cover and cook 2 to 3 hours or until beans are tender.

This soup can be frozen in batches or individual servings. It makes a hearty meal or first course. Some prefer this type of soup to be a very smooth texture. You may want to blend or puree small batches in a blender or food processor to desired consistency. Garnish with a dolop of plain yogurt.

Makes 6 servings.

Each serving contains:
- *170 calories*
- *9 grams protein*
- *29 grams carbohydrate*
- *negligible grams fat*
- *37 mg. sodium*
- *0 mg. cholesterol*
- *12 grams fiber*

ADA Exchange Value
- *2 Starch*
- *negligible fat calories.*

Chicken Gumbo

6 cups Chicken Broth (page 124)
12 oz. chicken, cooked and skinned
2 large stalks celery, sliced
1 small green pepper, seeded and chopped
1 medium onion, chopped
1 16 oz. can tomatoes, low salt type preferred
2 cups frozen or fresh cut okra
2 tablespoons quick cooking tapioca
1 teaspoon thyme
2 bay leaves
$1/8$ teaspoon cayenne pepper
3 cups cooked brown rice

1. Spray a heavy soup pot with nonstick spray. Saute celery, green pepper, onion and okra just until tender.
2. Add tomatoes, tapioca, thyme, bay leaves and cayenne pepper.
3. Add chicken and Chicken Broth. Bring to a boil, then quickly reduce heat and simmer for about 30 minutes.
4. Serve in a soup bowl over brown rice.

Makes 6 servings.

Each serving contains:
146 calories
15 grams protein
17 grams carbohydrate
2 grams fat
46 mg. sodium
33 mg. cholesterol
3 grams fiber

ADA Exchange Value
2 Lean Meat
1 Starch
14% of total calories are from fat.

Red Beans and Rice

$^1/_2$ **pound red beans, soaked in water overnight and rinsed**
   1 **medium onion, chopped**
   1 **cup celery, chopped fine**
   1 **cup green pepper, chopped fine**
   1 **teaspoon Tabasco**
   1 **teaspoon white pepper**
   1 **teaspoon ground thyme**
$^1/_2$ **teaspoon garlic powder**
$^1/_2$ **teaspoon ground cayenne pepper**
$^1/_4$ **teaspoon ground black pepper**
   2 **bay leaves**
   2 **cups cooked brown rice**
   2 **cups fresh, chopped tomatoes**

1. In a Dutch oven sprayed with a nonstick spray, saute onion, celery and bell pepper until soft. Add Tabasco, white, black and cayenne pepper, thyme and garlic. Mix in well.
2. Add red beans. Cover with water. Add bay leaves, cover and simmer until done (stir occasionally adding more water if necessary).
3. Remove bay leaves.
4. Take out 2 cups of beans including liquid. Puree in blender and return to pot.
5. Serve beans over rice or mix together. Garnish with tomatoes.

Makes 8 servings.

Each serving contains:
   156 calories
      7 grams protein
     31 grams carbohydrate
          negligible grams fat
     11 mg. sodium

0   mg. cholesterol
9   grams fiber

    ADA Exchange Value
2   Starch
    negligible fat calories.

Creole Corn

1   cup whole kernel corn, fresh or frozen
1   cup cut okra, fresh or frozen
1   cup canned tomatoes, low salt type preferred
*   dash of cayenne pepper*

1. Place all ingredients in a small sauce pan.
2. Heat slowly and simmer until done — about 10 minutes.
3. Serve in a small bowl as a side dish.

Makes 4 servings.

Each serving contains:
*   66   calories*
*   3   grams protein*
*   15   grams carbohydrate*
*   negligible grams fat*
*   16   mg. sodium*
*   0   mg. cholesterol*
*   4   grams fiber*

*   ADA Exchange Value*
*   1   Starch*
*   negligible fat calories.*

Dirty Rice

This is a great one-dish meal. You can also take the basic concept of the dish and use your leftovers in it. This is a good dish to make in your rice cooker.

1	*teaspoon ground cayenne pepper*
1	*teaspoon ground black pepper*
1 1/4	*teaspoon sweet paprika*
1/2	*teaspoon dry mustard*
1/2	*teaspoon ground cumin*
1/2	*teaspoon ground thyme*
2	*bay leaves*
1	*medium onion, chopped*
1	*clove garlic, chopped*
1	*pound chicken breast, skinned, boned and cut into cubes*
1	*cup brown rice, uncooked*
2 1/2	*cups low salt chicken broth*

1. Mix spices together except for bay leaves. Set aside.
2. In a Dutch oven sprayed with a nonstick spray, saute onion and garlic until soft. Add the spices and saute for 30 seconds.
3. Add chicken cubes and saute 1 minute, stirring constantly.
4. Add rice, chicken broth and bay leaves. Bring to a boil. Reduce heat to simmer. Cover and cook 45 minutes or put in a 350 degree oven for 45 minutes.
4. Before serving, remove bay leaves.

Makes 4 servings.

Each serving contains:

- *221 calories*
- *27 grams protein*
- *17 grams carbohydrate*
- *4 grams fat*
- *321 mg. sodium*
- *67 mg. cholesterol*
- *1 gram fiber*

ADA Exchange Value

- *3 Lean Meat*
- *1 Starch*
- *18% of total calories are from fat.*

Jambalaya Salad

1 cup Chicken Broth (page 124)
1/4 cup tomato sauce, no salt type preferred
1/4 cup onion, finely chopped
1/4 cup celery, finely chopped
1/2 cup brown rice, uncooked
1/2 teaspoon basil
1/4 teaspoon oregano
1/2 teaspoon chervil
1/2 teaspoon paprika
1/2 teaspoon dry mustard
1/4 teaspoon cayenne pepper
1/4 cup white vinegar
1/4 cup Chicken Broth (page 124)
2 tablespoons oil
2 cloves garlic, pressed
8 oz. cooked shrimp
1 head lettuce

1. Heat 1 cup broth, tomato sauce, onion and celery to boil. Stir in rice, then cover and cook over low heat about 40 minutes or until done. Stir to fluff lightly, then chill.
2. Combine basil, oregano, chervil, paprika, dry mustard, cayenne pepper, vinegar, 1/4 cup Chicken Broth, oil and garlic into a jar. Cover and shake well to blend. Pour over cooked shrimp, cover and refrigerate.
3. Shred lettuce and divide into 6 serving dishes or one large salad bowl. Arrange cooled rice on top of lettuce, then marinated shrimp on top of rice. Drizzle remaining dressing over rest of salad.

Makes 6 servings.

Each serving contains:

- *124 calories*
- *10 grams protein*
- *8 grams carbohydrate*
- *6 grams fat*
- *184 mg. sodium*
- *67 mg. cholesterol*
- *2 grams fiber*

ADA Exchange Value

- *1 Lean Meat*
- *$^1/_2$ Starch*
- *1 Fat*
- *41% of total calories are from fat.*

Jambalaya

Jambalaya is the answer to the Spanish paella, using spicier seasonings.

Pork Jambalaya

     1   *pound lean pork loin, cubed*
     2   *medium onions, chopped*
1 1/2   *cups celery chopped*
     1   *clove garlic, chopped*
     1   *teaspoon ground white pepper*
     1   *teaspoon dry mustard*
     1   *teaspoon ground cayenne pepper*
   1/2   *teaspoon cumin*
   1/2   *teaspoon ground black pepper*
   1/2   *teaspoon ground thyme*
     2   *cups brown rice, uncooked*
     4   *cups low salt chicken broth*
     2   *bay leaves*

1. In a Dutch oven sprayed with a nonstick spray, brown the pork cubes. Take out of pan and set aside.
2. Put onions, celery and garlic in pan and cook until soft, stirring constantly.
3. Add seasonings to mixture and saute 30 seconds.
4. Return pork to pan, add brown rice, chicken broth and bay leaves. Bring to a boil.
5. Cover and reduce to a simmer and cook 50 minutes, or place in a 350 degree oven for 1 hour.

Serves 8.

Each serving contains:

- 180 *calories*
- 16 *grams protein*
- 14 *grams carbohydrate*
- 7 *grams fat*
- 52 *mg. sodium*
- 45 *mg. cholesterol*
- 1 *gram fiber*

ADA Exchange Value

- 2 *Lean Meat*
- 1 *Starch*
- $^1/_2$ *Fat*
- 34% *of total calories are from fat.*

Chicken Gizzard Jambalaya

- 1 *pound chicken gizzards, trimmed of gristle and diced*
- 8 *oz. boned and skinned chicken thighs, cubed*
- 1 *medium onion, chopped*
- 1 *cup celery, chopped*
- 1 *cup carrots, chopped*
- 1 1/2 *teaspoon ground white pepper*
- 1 *teaspoon ground pepper*
- 1 *teaspoon ground thyme*
- 1/2 *teaspoon ground sage*
- 1 *15 oz. can diced tomatoes in juice*
- 2 *cups brown rice, uncooked*
- 1 1/2 *cups low salt chicken broth*
- 2 *bay leaves*

1. In aDutch oven sprayed with a nonstick spray, brown gizzards and thighs. Remove from pan and set aside.
2. Add onion, celery and carrots to pan. Saute until soft. Add seasonings and saute 30 seconds.
3. Add tomatoes and juice, rice and chicken broth to pan. Return chicken to pan and bring to a boil. Add bay leaves. Cover and cook 50 minutes or put in 350 degree oven for 1 hour.

Makes 8 servings.

Each serving contains:

164	*calories*
16	*grams protein*
19	*grams carbohydrate*
3	*grams fat*
154	*mg. sodium*
118	*mg. cholesterol*
3	*grams fiber*

ADA Exchange Value

1 1/2	*Lean Meat*
1	*Starch*
1	*Vegetable*
15%	*of total calories are from fat.*

Creole Sauce

1 **medium onion, chopped**
1/2 **green pepper, seeded and chopped**
1 **large stalk celery, chopped**
1 **pound can tomatoes, no salt added**
1/4 **teaspoon black pepper**
1 **cup Chicken Broth (page 124)**
1/8 **teaspoon cayenne pepper or few drops hot pepper sauce**

1. Spray a skillet with nonstick spray. Saute onion, green pepper and celery until tender.
2. Add tomatoes, black pepper, cayenne pepper and Chicken Broth. Simmer for a few minutes or until sauce has reduced down and thickened slightly.

Use this sauce for Chicken Creole (page 203) or as a base for Gumbo (page 190).

Makes 4 servings.

Each serving contains:
    40 *calories*
    2 *grams protein*
    8 *grams carbohydrate*
    negligible grams fat
    534 *mg. sodium*
    negligible mg. cholesterol
    2 *grams fiber*

    ADA Exchange Value
    2 *Vegetable*
    14% *of total calories are from fat.*

Chicken Creole

1 recipe Creole Sauce (page 202)
1 pound raw chicken breasts, boned and skinned
2 cups cooked rice (brown rice preferred)

1. Place chicken breasts in a skillet. Add enough water to barely cover. Add bay leaf and bring to a boil. Immediately reduce to a simmer and poach chicken until tender. Do not boil.
2. Have Creole Sauce and rice hot. Place 1/2 cup of rice on a plate. Place chicken breast on top. Then cover with 1/4 recipe of Creole Sauce.

Makes 4 servings.

Each serving contains:

287	*calories*
29	*grams protein*
33	*grams carbohydrate*
4	*grams fat*
591	*mg. sodium*
66	*mg. cholesterol*
3	*grams fiber*

ADA Exchange Value

3	*Lean Meat*
2	*Starch*
13%	*of total calories are from fat.*

Spicy Apricot Dijon Chicken

4 chicken breasts, skinned
1/4 cup low calorie or low sugar apricot jam
2 tablespoons Dijon mustard
1/8 teaspoon cayenne pepper

1. Preheat oven to 350 degrees.
2. Place chicken breasts in a small baking dish.
3. Combine apricot jam, mustard and cayenne pepper
4. Pour or spoon jam mixture over chicken. Cover loosely with foil and bake about 35 to 45 minutes or until done.

Makes 4 servings.

Each serving contains:
- 212 calories
- 33 grams protein
- 7 grams carbohydrate
- 5 grams fat
- 171 mg. sodium
- 88 mg. cholesterol
- negligible grams fiber

ADA Exchange Value
- 4 Lean Meat
- 1/2 Fruit
- 20% of total calories are from fat.

Cajun Oven Fried Chicken

4 **chicken breasts, skinned**
1/4 **cup buttermilk**
2 **tablespoons flour**
2 **tablespoons cornmeal**
1/4 **teaspoon oregano**
1/4 **teaspoon marjoram**
1/8 **teaspoon paprika**
1/8 **teaspoon cayenne pepper**

1. Preheat oven to 350 degrees.
2. Place chicken breasts in a dish and pour buttermilk over them, turning to coat well.
3. Combine flour, cornmeal, oregano, marjoram, paprika and cayenne pepper. Put mixture into a bag or large flat dish.
4. Coat each piece of chicken with flour mixture. Then place chicken onto a cookie sheet that has been sprayed with nonstick spray.
5. Bake, uncovered at 350 degrees for 35 to 45 minutes or until done.

Makes 4 servings.

Each serving contains:
    215 **calories**
     34 **grams protein**
      7 **grams carbohydrate**
      5 **grams fat**
     88 **mg. sodium**
     89 **mg. cholesterol**
         negligible grams fiber

        ADA Exchange Value
      4 **Lean Meat**
    1/2 **Starch**
    20% **of total calories are from fat.**

Blackened Fish

Blackened food has become one of the most popular items in the Cajun cuisine. The traditional method of preparation is to cook it at a very high heat with lots of clarified butter. By eliminating that and broiling, BBQ or cooking it in the skillet with a nonstick spray makes it a very healthy and tasty dish.

> **2 pounds fish (red fish, halibut, swordfish, salmon or shrimp)**

Seasoning Mix
> **1 teaspoon paprika**
> **1 teaspoon onion powder**
> **1 teaspoon cayenne pepper**
> **$^1/_4$ teaspoon ground white pepper**
> **$^1/_2$ teaspoon ground thyme**

1. Mix all seasonings together.
2. Rub seasoning mix on both sides of fish.
3. Cook either under broiler, BBQ or saute in nonstick skillet until done (each fish will have a different cooking time, but keep in mind that fish cooks quickly).

Makes 6 servings.

Each serving contains:
> **124 calories**
> **23 grams protein**
> **negligible grams carbohydrate**
> **3 grams fat**
> **61 mg. sodium**
> **36 mg. cholesterol**
> **negligible grams fiber**

> **ADA Exchange Value**
> **3 Lean Meat**
> **18% of total calories are from fat.**

Guiltless Bananas Foster

This is a calorie-reduced version of the famous recipe served at Brennen's in New Orleans.

> 1 *tablespoon margarine*
> 2 *tablespoons fructose*
> 1/2 *teaspoon banana extract*
> 1 *teaspoon rum extract*
> 2 *medium bananas, peeled, cut in half lengthwise, then quartered*
> 1 *pint low calorie ice cream*

1. Using a medium-sized, heavy skillet, melt margarine but do not brown.
2. Add fructose and allow to melt. Stir well when melted. Makes a slightly thickened syrup. Add extracts carefully as they will spatter.
3. Add the 8 banana quarters and brown on each side.
4. Serve over ice cream or nonfat yogurt. Spoon a little sauce over each serving.

Makes 4 servings.

Each serving contains:

> 169 *calories*
> 3 *grams protein*
> 28 *grams carbohydrate*
> 6 *grams fat*
> 53 *mg. sodium*
> 9 *mg. cholesterol*
> 1 *gram fiber*

> *ADA Exchange Value*
> 2 *Fruit*
> 1 *Fat*
> 31% *of total calories are from fat.*

Peach Crisp

2 **cups sliced peaches, about 3 to 4 medium peaches**
1/4 **cup flour**
1/4 **cup graham cracker crumbs, 4 squares crushed**
2 **tablespoons fructose**
2 **tablespoons margarine**
1/2 **teaspoon cinnamon**

1. Preheat oven to 375 degrees.
2. Place sliced peaches into 9x9x2 inch pan or baking dish. Sprinkle with 1 tablespoon fructose.
3. Combine flour, graham cracker crumbs, cinnamon and 1 tablespoon fructose. Cut in margarine until crumbly.
4. Sprinkle mixture evenly over top of peaches.
5. Bake at 375 degrees for 30 minutes.

Makes 4 servings.

Each serving contains:
153 *calories*
2 *grams protein*
24 *grams carbohydrate*
6 *grams fat*
55 *mg. sodium*
0 *mg. cholesterol*
1 *gram fiber*

ADA Exchange Value
1/2 *Starch*
1 *Fruit*
1 *Fat*
38% *of total calories are from fat.*

Sweet Potato Custard

1 1/2   **cups fresh cooked sweet potato**
1   **cup nonfat milk**
1/4   **cup fresh orange juice**
1   **tablespoon orange peel**
1/2   **teaspoon nutmeg**
1/4   **cup fructose**
4   **egg whites**

1. Combine all ingredients in a blender and blend until smooth.
2. Pour mixture into a 1-quart baking dish or into 6 individual custard cups. Place baking dish or custard cups into a water bath and bake at 350 degrees about 30 minutes or until center has set. Cool, then chill well before serving.

Makes 6 servings.

Each serving contains:
  59 *calories*
  4 *grams protein*
  11 *grams carbohydrate*
    negligible grams fat
  65 *mg. sodium*
    negligible mg. cholesterol
    negligible grams fiber

    ADA Exchange Value
  1/2 *Starch*
  1/2 *Fruit*
    negligible fat calories.

Rice Pudding

This Rice Pudding comes from a family recipe that has always been a favorite. It is a milky-type pudding — not firm.

> 1 **cup cooked brown rice**
> 2 **tablespoons fructose**
> 1 **teaspoon vanilla**
> 1/4 **teaspoon cinnamon**
> 2 **cups 1% milk, scalded**
> **fresh grated nutmeg**

1. Preheat oven to 300 degrees.
2. Place rice in a 1-quart baking dish and stir in cinnamon.
3. Combine fructose and vanilla with scalded milk and pour into dish with rice.
4. Grate fresh nutmeg over top and bake 1 1/2 hours or until a firm "skin" appears on the top. Cool before serving.

Makes 4 servings.

Each serving contains:
> 98 **calories**
> 5 **grams protein**
> 16 **grams carbohydrate**
> 2 **grams fat**
> 69 **mg. sodium**
> 5 **mg. cholesterol**
> **negligible grams fiber**
>
> **ADA Exchange Value**
> 1/2 **Starch**
> 1/2 **1% Milk**
> 14% **of total calories are from fat.**

Bread Pudding

6   egg whites
$^3/_4$ cup fructose
1$^1/_2$ teaspoon vanilla extract
1   teaspoon ground nutmeg
1   teaspoon ground cinnamon
1   tablespoon Butter Buds™, dry
2   cups 1% milk
$^1/_2$ cup raisins
$^1/_2$ cup chopped pecans
5   cups very stale french bread with crust, cut in 1/2-inch cubes
1   cup Yogurt Cream (page 213)

1. In a large bowl, whip egg whites, slowly adding the fructose until soft peaks form.
2. Mix vanilla, nutmeg, cinnamon and Butter Buds™ into milk.
3. Add raisins and pecans to milk mixture. Pour over bread cubes.
4. Fold the bread cube mixture into egg whites. Let stand 25 minutes.
5. Pour mixture into a loaf pan sprayed with a nonstick spray. Let stand 20 minutes more.
6. Place into a preheated oven at 350 degrees, lower heat to 300 degrees, bake 40 minutes, then increase temperature to 425 degrees and bake 15 minutes.
7. Divide mixture into 8 serving dishes and top each with 2 tablespoons Yogurt Cream.

Makes 8 servings.

Each serving contains:

- 251 *calories*
- 9 *grams protein*
- 40 *grams carbohydrate*
- 7 *grams fat*
- 246 *mg. sodium*
- 4 *mg. cholesterol*
- 2 *grams fiber*

ADA Exchange Value

- 1 **Starch**
- 1 1/2 **Fruit**
- 1/2 **Lean Meat**
- 1 **Fat**
- 23% *of total calories are from fat.*

Yogurt Cream

This is a no-fat topping that is excellent on top of desserts of fruit to give it just that little something extra!

> 1 **cup Yogurt Cheese (page 214)**
> ³/₄ **teaspoon vanilla**
> 4 **packages Equal™**

Mix all ingredients together and store in refrigerator in a covered container until ready to use.

Makes 8 servings.

Each serving contains:
- 21 *calories*
- 2 *grams protein*
- 2 *grams carbohydrate*
- *negligible grams fat*
- 20 *mg. sodium*
- 0 *mg. cholesterol*
- 0 *grams fiber*

ADA Exchange Value

negligible fat calories.

Yogurt Cheese

This is an excellent nonfat replacement for high-fat items —
cream cheese, mayonnaise or sour cream. You can make it into
a sweet cream or a spicy dip!

> **16   oz. plain nonfat yogurt, without any added
> gelatin**

1. Place yogurt in a colander lined with coffee filters. Place in a
   bowl and cover top. Refrigerate for 18 to 24 hours.
2. Throw out liquid and store Yogurt Cheese in a covered
   container until ready to use.

Makes 8 oz.

Each serving contains:
- *225   calories*
- *24   grams protein*
- *32   grams carbohydrate*
- *negligible grams fat*
- *150   mg. sodium*
- *0   mg. cholesterol*
- *0   grams fiber*

> *ADA Exchange Value*
> *2   Nonfat Milk*
> *negligible fat calories.*

INDEX

Recipe Notes

Recipe Notes

ABOUT THE AUTHORS

Judy Gilliard and Joy Kirkpatrick are a perfectly paired partnership. Together they have used bushels of imagination and a delightfully fresh approach to healthful food preparation.

Judy, who holds a degree in restaurant management, has been a restaurant consultant and an instructor in the same field. She is trained in classical French methods of cuisine.

A few years ago, Judy was diagnosed as a diet-controlled (type II) diabetic. Her diet "prescription" included a low-fat, low-salt, low-cholesterol regimen. She was encouraged to include fresh fruits, vegetables and whole grain products in her diet.

Judy was faced with new dietary requirements, and the knowledge that her health and daily well-being depended on these requirements. She met and consulted with Joy Kirkpatrick, a Registered Dietitian and Certified Diabetes Educator, specializing in diabetes education since 1976.

Trained in the art of and still loving gourmet cooking, Judy set out to find ways to make her diet taste exciting and anything but bland.

Stating that she'd always wanted to write cookbooks, Judy then spoke with Joy about collaborating on a cookbook for health-conscious people.

From that simple idea sprang a wonderful book of delicious, gourmet recipes called *The Guiltless Gourmet*.

The best of their recipes were presented for dieters, diabetics, individuals on sodium- or cholesterol-restricted diets and for anyone interested in sound nutrition and creative cookery!

Now the pair has added *The Guiltless Gourmet Goes Ethnic*!

When not working on recipes for *The Guiltless Gourmet Series*, Joy spends her time in private practice as a consultant to various facilities and programs in Southern California's Coachella Valley.

She is a member of both the American Dietetic Association and the American Diabetes Association. She was on the editorial committee for the revision of the American Diabetes Association cookbook, has taught nutrition at the community college level, participated in numerous seminars in weight control and the importance of diet in good health maintenance.

Joy has contributed articles to Forecast Magazine, and currently serves as a board member of the Desert Chapter of the American Heart Association. Joy is a Clinical Dietitian at John F. Kennedy Memorial Hospital in Indio, California, where her duties include teaching out-patient diabetes education classes as well as participating in a diabetes and pregnancy program. She is also co-host of a weekly radio talk show on health and nutrition.

Judy is Vice President/General Manager for KPSI Radio Corporation in Palm Springs, California. She also adds to her credentials a membership with the American Food and Wine Institute, The International Association of Cooking Professionals and serves on the board of the American Heart Association and the Palm Springs Chamber of Commerce.

If you found this book helpful and would like more information on this and other related subjects, you may be interested in one or more of the following titles from DCI Publishing.

BOOKS

Fast Food Facts, 3rd Edition: Nutrition and Exchange Values for Fast Food Restaurants (200 pages)

Fast Food Facts, pocket edition (184 pages)

Making the Most of Medicare: A Personal Guide Through the Medicare Maze (170 pages)

Fight Fat & Win: How to Eat a Low-Fat Diet Without Changing Your Lifestyle

The Guiltless Gourmet Cooks Ethnic: Low-Fat EthnicRecipes, Menus & Nutrition Facts (250 pages)

When a Family Get Diabetes: Art therapy to help kids and families understand diabetes (50 pages)

Expresslane Diet: Weight Loss with Convenience and Fast Foods (176 pages)

Retirement: New Beginnings, New Challenges, New Successes (140 pages)

Whole Parent/Whole Child: Raising a Chronically Ill Child (175 pages)

Diabetes: A Guide to Living Well: A Program of Individualized Self-Care (396 pages)

Adult Braces in a Gourmet World: A Consumer's Guide to Straight Teeth (148 pages)

I Can Cope: Staying Healthy with Cancer (202 pages)

Managing the School Age Child with a Chronic Health Condition (350 pages)

Pass the Pepper Please: Healthy Meal Planning with Low Sodium (66 pages)

The Guiltless Gourmet: Recipes, Menus for the Health Conscious Cook (170 pages)

The Joy of Snacks: Good Nutrition for People Who Like to Snack (270 pages)

Convenience Food Facts: Help for the Healthy Meal Planner (188 pages)

Learning to Live Well With Diabetes: Your Complete Guide to Diabetes Management 9392 pages)

The Physician Within: Taking Charge of Your Well-Being (170 pages)

Exchanges for All Occasions: Meeting the Challenge of Diabetes and Weight Control (250 pages)

Managing Type II Diabetes: Your Invitation to a Healthier Lifestyle (170 pages)

Diabetes 101: A Pure and Simple Guide for People Who Use Insulin (110 pages)

DCI Publishing is the publishing division of Diabetes Center, Inc., publishers of quality educational materials dealing with health, wellness, nutrition, diabetes, and other chronic illnesses. All our books and materials are available nationwide and in Canada through leading bookstores. If you can't find our books at your favorite bookstore, contact us directly for a free catalog.

DCI Publishing, Inc.
P.O. Box 47945
Minneapolis, MN 55447-9727